A heart stirring devotional you'll want to read like a novel, *My Mother's Quilts* is rich in the kind of history that makes you long for a simpler time. It's steeped in inspiration from faith handed down from one generation to another and seasoned with application that stirred my heart to prayer and praise.

Ane Mulligan, President Novel Rocket,
author of *Chapel Springs Revival*

The fabric of legacy—those words sum up this amazing devotional by Ramona Richards. Together with images from generations of quilts, she pieces together family stories, Scripture, and insight to produce a patchwork of encouragement and comfort. *My Mother's Quilts* will hold a forever place on my nightstand.

Edie Melson, Author of *While My Soldier Serves*
and *While My Child Is Away*

Through the intricate quilt patterns and simple but compelling faith of the strong women who form her ancestry, Ramona Richards traces the meaning of legacy in the pages of *My Mother's Quilts*. This memoir/devotional not only celebrates the women and art they made through quilts, but the truth that "our ancestors influenced us in many unseen ways, just as we will influence those who come after us."

Cynthia Ruchti, Speaker and author of award-winning books
including *All My Belongings* and *As Waters Gone By*

Our memories often help define who we are. And tangible objects can bring those memories to life. *My Mother's Quilts* offers us the chance to slip back in time, remembering the women who have been so influential in our lives. And the beauty of the quilts weaves the memories, bright with colors, bright with recollections so real the folks live again in our hearts. *My Mother's Quilts* offers heart-changing devotions so real you can touch the colorful stitching.

Linda S. Glaz, Multi-published author
and literary agent

Ramona Richards's latest book is made from timeless swatches of nostalgia carefully pieced and lovingly sewn together by a master storyteller. You will surely, as I have, create a long list of those you wish to read this treasure.

Eva Marie Everson, Best-selling author of
fiction and nonfiction works

In *My Mother's Quilts*, Ramona Richards stitches together a charming collection of family stories, devotional thoughts, and the fascinating history of the quilts in her family. Your heart will feel as warm as if you've had one of those quilts tucked around you. I loved reading this book!

Michelle Cox, author of *Just 18 Summers* and
God Glimpses from the Jewelry Box

My Mother's Quilts

Devotions of Love, Legacy, Family, and Faith

My Mother's Quilts

Devotions of Love, Legacy, Family, and Faith

Ramona Richards

WORTHY®
Inspired

ISBN 978-1-61795-612-6

Published by Worthy Inspired, an imprint of Worthy Publishing Group, a division of Worthy Media, Inc., One Franklin Park, 6100 Tower Circle, Suite 210, Franklin, TN 37067.
WORTHY is a registered trademark of Worthy Media, Inc.

HELPING PEOPLE EXPERIENCE THE HEART OF GOD

Names: Richards, Ramona, 1957-
Title: My mother's quilts : devotions of love, legacy, family, and faith /
    Ramona Richards.
Description: Franklin, TN : Worthy Pub., 2015.
Identifiers: LCCN 2015037824 | ISBN 9781617956126 (hardcover)
Subjects: LCSH: Quiltmakers--Religious life. | Quilting--Miscellanea. | Pope,
    Jimmie Lou Waldrop, 1926-2014. | Mothers and daughters--Religious
    aspects--Christianity. | Richards, Ramona, 1957-
Classification: LCC BV4596.N44 R53 2015 | DDC 242--dc23
LC record available at http://lccn.loc.gov/2015037824

Cover Design by Jeffery Jansen / Aesthetic Soup
All photos by Mary Smith, Mary Mason Photography, www.marymasonphotography.com, except photos of the Log Cabin quilt, courtesy of William Ray Pope.

Printed in China
1 2 3 4 5 6 7 RRD 20 19 18 17 16

Contents

- -

A NOTE TO THE READER ON
MEMORIES AND QUILT PATTERNS

I talked to my mother a lot about quilting over the years. In fact, she talked quilting with anyone who would listen. The memories mentioned in this book, however, are my own. Most of these events and conversations happened when Mother and I were alone, but other moments involved an entire community of relatives and friends. Their perceptions may vary somewhat, as is the nature of memories and observations. But they have been supportive and encouraging about the writing of this book as a way to preserve the heritage of needlework that has been woven throughout our history. Most of the women in my family, as far back as we can trace, were quilters, either out of love or necessity.

For my mother, quilting was an art and craft she adopted with a passion. She showed me pattern after pattern; some she planned to work on, others that were in process, and a few she only dreamed of attempting. She collected hundreds from books, friends, newspapers, and magazines. She adapted more than one to whatever fabric she had or size she needed. For others, the special creations, she went shopping for bolts and fat quarters—bundles, those wide-cut quarter yards of fabric that quilters prize. She met regularly with a quilters' guild in Hartselle, Alabama, and they traded and swapped even more.

I don't remember all the names. I don't remember which ones she altered to her own designs. Mostly I remember the love, the care for details, the respect for the craft, and the memories surrounding each quilt. And although some of her quilts were tagged with the name of the quilter and the pattern, many of the tags just included the quiltmaker, location, and year. My cousin, Rebecca Mason Thomas, and I have researched and queried and scoured the Internet, but some of the patterns named in this book are just our best guesses based on our research. I'd love to hear from anyone who knows an alternative name for the patterns.

Introduction

FAITH, HOPE, AND LOVE IN EVERY BLOCK

When my mother and I sat down to make plans for her funeral, we decided to use one of her quilts on the casket instead of a blanket of flowers. She chose her Butterfly Handkerchief quilt, which featured her own mother's handkerchiefs. My grandmother carried a handkerchief everywhere she went, especially to church. Being too poor to purchase such a luxury, my grandmother made her own from any available fabric. She'd add embroidery or tat lace for the edges, although some bold prints and colors needed little more than hemming. When my grandmother died, Mother took those treasured squares and transformed each into a lovely butterfly, centered on a twelve-inch quilt block. The quilted stitches around the outside of the quilt formed their own line of precise butterflies.

It was one of my mother's most cherished quilts. It stayed on display in her living room until she went into an assisted living facility. When I'd visit her home, our conversation would frequently drift to the quilt, and she'd share the story of one of the handkerchiefs—what the fabric had been used for originally or a special time she remembered

1

my grandmother carrying a particular one. That spurred us to talk about the other quilts she owned.

My mother was a master quilter. It was her passion and great love. She belonged to a local guild and took trips to quilt shows. She constantly read about them, and she sought out the history of patterns and fabrics. Although Mother pieced most of her quilts on a machine, every quilted stitch was by hand, and she enjoyed finding different stitching stencils to add pizzazz to her work.

But Mother also owned a number of quilts that had been passed down to her from her mother, grandmother, and assorted friends and relatives. She even owned a quilt pieced in North Carolina during the 1830s and transported over the mountains into Alabama when our family migrated west. Once a brilliant red-and-green Carolina Lily pattern, the antebellum quilt survived the Civil War by being buried in a barn. The years underground left it a faded brown and rusty orange, but it was still intact, if fragile, after almost 180 years. After much discussion with my brother and me, Mother donated it to her hometown museum.

It weighed on her, however, that the story of the Carolina Lily quilt, and all the others, would soon be forgotten. No one but her knew their tales. So she stitched a white fabric tag to the back of most of the quilts, on which she wrote as much as she knew about the quilt's origins. And she began to share with me the stories behind each one, accounts that not only described the beginning of a quilt but the ongoing legacy of the seamstresses in her life—their faith, their hopes for the future, their dreams, their adventures.

When the time finally came to use the Butterfly Handkerchief quilt on her casket, all those stories came rushing back to me as people asked me, repeatedly, about the quilt. I used it in her eulogy, explaining how important to her it had been not to lose the fabric of my grandmother's life and legacy. How important it was to preserve those elements of character and grace far beyond her time here on earth. After Mother's funeral, the quilt became the center of attention, as family gathered around. Some of the cousins there I had not seen in decades, but we were suddenly united by a quilt—what it stood for and what it meant to all of us.

It was a reminder that all families have such treasure embedded in their weaving, and I knew I had to share the lessons I had learned from my mother's stories of seamstresses past and present. Quilts and other needlework—once necessities—now make up our legacy of faith and hope. Whether they're a 180-year-old Carolina Lily quilt, 75-year-old handkerchiefs, or a 25-year-old Butterfly Handkerchief quilt, the stitches of our family are very much like our faith: They bind us, comfort us, and help us share the foundations of the past with the generations of the future.

Grandmother
Omie Brothers Pope,
Ray, and Ramona
(circa 1959)

Granddaddy
Rother Waldrop,
Grandmother Ila Harp
Waldrop, Mother,
Ramona, and Ray
(circa 1958)

My Mother,
Jimmie Lou
Waldrop Pope
(circa 1948)

Mother with the
Carolina Lily quilt
(circa 1990)

A Faded Pattern

CAROLINA LILY

- -

She selects wool and flax and works with eager hands.

Proverbs 31:13

- -

T he fabric definitely dates to the 1830s or 1840s."

I watched my cousin Becky carefully run white-gloved hands over the vintage quilt, comparing the cloth to examples in one of her books on the history of fabrics. The faded quilt, tattered and worn around the edges, lay spread over the museum table. It doesn't look like much compared to modern quilts, with their brilliant colors and innovative patterns. The colors of the familiar Carolina Lily pattern have paled from bright red and green to orange and brown. The white background is now umber. It is smaller than recently made quilts, built for narrow mattresses of corn shucks or straw.

Becky paused over one square. "Here." She pointed. "That one only appeared in that decade. And the wool batting puts it pre-Civil War." The handwoven back places its construction in North Carolina, confirming the family stories of the young couple who trusted God with an unknown future on the other side of the mountains. It even comes with its own legend: In order to keep it from being confiscated by marauders and soldiers alike, it spent the Civil War buried in a trunk in the barn, along with some other valuables.

After the war, it wasn't used much, but it was passed down from one woman to the next. My grandmother would take it out each year, air it over an outside clothesline, then

lovingly pack it away, sharing the age-old tales about the quilt as she did so. Stories of love, faith, and sacrifice, such as most families have dotting their past.

By the time my mother received it, it had deteriorated too much for restoration, so the family made the decision to wrap it in acid-free paper, in an equally acid-free box, and donate it to the St. Clair County (Alabama) Museum and Archives, where it's displayed occasionally, a marker of the area's history.

But it's far more than that. It's a faded symbol of something that never fades. While we cherish the Carolina Lily because it's a legacy of our handicraft, it's also a reminder that faith and family, and a belief that God will take care of us, endure in the same way: passed down to the next generation.

PRAYER STARTER

- - - - - - - - - - - - -

Father, You have blessed Your children across thousands of years and shown them how to disciple and love their own. Guide me as I pass my faith to a new generation of believers. Amen.

One Woman's Trash

DUTCH DOLL

- -

Bless all his skills, LORD,
and be pleased with the work of his hands.

Deuteronomy 33:11

- -

My mother held a distinct measure of pride in most of her quilts. After all, a lot of hours and hard work went into them. The one exception to this was a Dutch Doll quilt, which she'd made and presented to me on my eighteenth birthday. I had already been accepted into my college of choice, and she made the quilt for my dorm room bed. It was the first quilt she had made, when she was just beginning to quilt seriously again. It was an experiment of sorts. When she'd finished it a few months before, she'd been pleased with it, as it represented an accomplishment of a new hobby—and a new phase—in her life. As a first effort, it was quite good.

I adored that quilt. I used it as a bedspread, and eagerly pointed out to friends that the "dolls" on it had been fashioned from clothes I'd worn in high school. Mother had embellished each doll with embroidery, and the bright colors livened up the dorm room.

Problems arose, though, as Mother learned more about quilting and appropriate fabrics to use. She started spotting the flaws in the quilt, which aggravated her more and more every time I brought the quilt home for the summer. She'd made the dolls from double knit, whereas the rest of the cloth was bleached cotton. This is a no-no in quilting as the two fabrics wear and shrink at different rates. The stitching wasn't straight because she hadn't lined out the pattern properly. The embroidery was sloppy. In fact, the more she learned, the more problems she found with the Dutch Doll.

She begged me to let her make me another one, stitched from her newly acquired information, but I refused. I wanted *that* one. And I used it until the stitching wore out.

When finally a portion of it needed to be requilted, she tried one last time to talk me into another quilt. I finally told her, "I don't care about the craft of quilting. I care that you made this especially for me. That you made it from my old clothes, the same clothes you'd sewn for me in high school. For me, it's not about the quilting. It's about the quilt and the fact that you made it."

She relented and completely repaired a quadrant of the quilt even though she felt it was trash. I didn't. To me, it was treasure.

I still own that quilt. It reminds me that love may see the flaws in others, but those flaws don't matter. Love doesn't focus on the ways in which people do wrong, or on the mistakes they make. I think of all the lessons my mother learned and passed on to me while she was pursuing the craft of quilting, I'm encouraged to remember that though I'm not—and have never been—perfect, God loves me anyway.

My Dutch Doll quilt serves as a good reminder to me to look at others through the eyes of love. When I'm tempted to pick at and try to fix someone's flaws and imperfections, my mother's imperfect-but-treasured quilt reminds me that God sees us all as whole people, and that He wants us to experience the love and joy He felt when He created us.

And I believe that if we share with others what we've learned since the beginning of our walk of faith—in spite of or perhaps because of our imperfections—He'll be pleased with our handiwork, whatever shape it takes.

PRAYER STARTER

- - - - - - - - - - - - -

Lord, help me see the "whole" of the people
around me, not just the flaws or ripped seams.
Help me remember that they, too,
are Your children and beloved by You,
just as I am. Amen.

Welcoming Newcomers

TURTLE

- -

In Joppa there was a disciple named Tabitha (in Greek her name is Dorcas). Her life overflowed with good works and compassionate acts on behalf of those in need.

Acts 9:36 CEB

- -

The whole neighborhood called her Granny Bowlin, whether she was kin or not. She made an impression on everyone she knew, the young and the old, with her godly spirit and sweet nature. She was a quiltmaker out of necessity, as were most of the women of her generation, but her passion for quilting extended far beyond what was needed. She welcomed neighbors and new babies alike with one of her quilts. A lot of young couples called the street where she lived home in the late 1950s, folks who were just starting out in life and struggling to make ends meet. Men like my father often hitchhiked to work because owning a car cost too much. Everyone struggled, doing the best they could for their families. Granny, whose family had long since moved away, did what she could to help.

My brother and I both benefited from Granny Bowlin's generosity, although in slightly different ways. He received

a quilt that he still treasures and holds dear. I received a quilt top, a turtle quilt, its whimsical blocks the perfect gift for an active child. I received it unfinished, because we moved away before Granny could quilt it with the same fine stitches as she did my brother's. In hopes of bettering

things for his family, Daddy had taken a new job, which transferred us to a new city. Mother, caught up with two children and a new life among strangers, stored the turtles away in her cedar chest, set aside like so many other aspects of our former home.

And there it stayed until 1980, when my father's mother came to stay with us for a while. Grandmother Omie was loving, quick-witted, and active, but there wasn't much to do except read the Bible, which she did a lot. Home for the summer, I talked to her a lot about family and faith, but our conversations weren't enough to keep her engaged.

Then my mother suggested she quilt the turtles. Grandmother Omie embraced this—she'd known Granny Bowlin well, and she adored the idea of honoring her friend this way after all these years.

Quilting connected two women across a generation to each other and our family through a gift borne of love and generosity. Granny's original gift spread much further than she could have imagined. Like Dorcas, their good works reached far beyond their lifetimes. Sometimes, in a spirit of humility, we downplay the value of our works. But those around us will remember and cherish them.

PRAYER STARTER

- - - - - - - - - - - - -

Lord, keep me mindful of those around me whose works and generosity have blessed their families and friends. Help me repay them with love and support. Amen.

Passing It Along

POSTAGE STAMP

- -

Let all that you do be done with love.

1 Corinthians 16:14 NKJV

- -

My dad was only fourteen when his grandmother, Terah Maude Pope, died in 1940. The baby of his immediate family and the youngest of Terah's grandchildren, Daddy was towheaded and precocious, a favorite among relatives and neighbors alike. As a result, he'd often receive only an amused scolding for transgressions where his older siblings would have received more punishment. Cotton, his nickname since childhood because of his white-blond curls, ran freely through the small mountain community where he grew up, charming everyone with his wit and openness, his grandmother included.

The few pictures we have of Terah show a stern woman in modest clothing. But she cherished her family, holding them close. She made each one of the grandchildren a quilt, most of them like the one she stitched for my dad—intricate and colorful tops backed by feed sack muslin and filled with hand-carded cotton. The thread she used may have been handspun as well. Unlike other quilts we have from that era, this one is quilted with even and tiny stitches of dark thread.

Another reason I know Terah wasn't as solemn as the pictures is that all of the Popes love pranks and grand stories. Daddy and his siblings were no exception, and family gatherings always turned into a round-robin of stories, each one more outrageous than the last, all geared to exhaust everyone with laughter. Daddy's mom, who passed Terah's quilt to my mother, would try desperately to keep the stories modest and under control and would try to caution them. She'd wag a hand and scold, "Now, now, boys!" between bouts of laughter. It never worked. Storytelling was in their blood.

Terah's story, however, is in her quilt: a tale of hard work, frugality, and hardship. Her precise stitches tell us how insistent she was on doing things right. The intricacy of her quilt top reveals an artistic side. The squares of the Postage Stamp quilt are two inches across, conveying her willingness to spend hours collecting, clipping, and preparing a quilt that would last generations to come. To Terah, her grandson was worth the effort.

Like Terah, we never know if anything we do will have a lasting impact. Our world these days sometimes feels temporary, as if nothing will last for our children or grandchildren. But Scripture tells us that shouldn't be our concern. Our focus instead should be on acting out of love. When we hold those we love close, acting only for their benefit, God will take care of the rest.

PRAYER STARTER

Lord, help me maintain my focus on love, on working for those I care for, to show them Your way, no matter what I do. Amen.

What Goes Around

TRIP AROUND THE WORLD

- -

For I know the plans I have for you, declares the LORD,
plans for wholeness and not for evil,
to give you a future and a hope.

Jeremiah 29:11 ESV

- -

My memories of Mother's quilting date only back to the 1970s, after she took several sewing classes at a local adult education center. Her nest was almost empty, and bags of fabric began taking over any spare corner. She set up a quilting frame in our bonus room, and what started as a casual hobby became a passion.

But I later discovered that was not Mother's first quilting experience. After she married in 1947, she quit work to keep house for my dad . . . which consisted mainly of boredom. They lived in a garage apartment comprised of one small bedroom and a kitchen that she described as being "too small to swing a cat in." My mother always kept a spotless house, but this one took her about an hour a day to clean.

They didn't have much money, and post-war scarcities still reigned. To pass the time, Mother read long tomes like Lloyd C. Douglas's *The Robe* and Margaret Mitchell's *Gone with the Wind*, or visited with neighbors, which included her mother-in-law, my grandmother, Omie. They talked about everything—life, children, housekeeping, cooking, religion. Grandmother read the entire Bible at least once a year, and her King James Version was an old friend. Mother had been raised Southern Baptist, and Grandmother Omie was Nazarene; they had some intriguing chats. In the early years of her marriage, Mother was closer to her mother-in-law than she was to her own mom.

So it was that Grandmother Omie challenged her to make a new quilt for the marriage bed. Not an easy task, but Mother took it on. She'd grown up with two women, her mother and grandmother, who knew needlecraft inside and out, but Mother wanted to do this on her own. For months, she gathered feed and flour sacks from neighbors, cutting some of them into the strips that would become the Trip Around the World; the rest were bleached for the backing. She hand-carded the cotton batting from bolls picked on her father's farm. The stitching isn't even and the square corners don't always match up evenly, but it was sewn with love and helped create a lifelong bond with her mother-in-law. She also truly enjoyed the task, expressing her creativity with her needle.

Mother didn't quilt again for almost thirty years. My dad bought a truck, and she started traveling with him on his long hauls. Then my brother was born, and life began a long stretch of his frequent asthma attacks, moves to new cities, and another child. But that Trip Around the World quilt had planted a seed, and when her home was empty once again, she returned to her first love.

Scripture tells us that we never know what God has in store for our lives but that He'll prepare us for the journey. He plants people, tasks, and challenges before us with long-lasting impacts. When we follow His leading, God will guide us into an unknown future with a knowing hand.

PRAYER STARTER

- - - - - - - - - - - - -

Lord, I trust You. Help me remember that You have the best in mind for me, no matter the trials I must face to get there. Amen.

The Colors of the Past

DRESDEN PLATE

Read up on what happened before you were born;
dig into the past, understand your roots.
Ask your parents what it was like before you were born;
ask the old-ones, they'll tell you a thing or two.

Deuteronomy 32:7 MSG

The inferno of an Alabama summer can prepare a teenage girl for almost anything. Staying with my grandmother Ila felt a lot like camping. Her house had no air-conditioning, and window fans just moved the hot air from one room to another, doing little to cool the house until after dark. Even in the early '70s, she still had no inside bathroom, and the only running water was in the kitchen. Baths took place in large galvanized tubs, and, yes, I've done laundry in a wringer washer filled by buckets.

Because of the heat, we did as much of the gardening, cooking, and housework as possible in the early morning or late afternoon. We spent the scorching midday breaking beans, shucking corn . . . or quilting. Grandmother Ila set up a full-sized quilt frame in the living room, the coolest room in the house, and set an oscillating fan underneath. I would sometimes sit underneath the quilt as if it were a fort, letting the fan blow over me as I read comic books and novels from the local drugstore.

Whatever we were doing, we talked about faith and family. Who was doing well; who had messed up. How things used to be. I learned that her mother-in-law had been a midwife, and that her grandfather had been a soldier in the Civil War and a justice of the peace. A devout Southern Baptist, my grandmother had definite opinions about religion, which influenced me for years to come. She taught me to ask whatever questions I had about Jesus—and where to find the answers in Scripture.

She took on sewing for other folks, saving any fabric that was left over for quilts, handkerchiefs, place mats, and the like. Her mind never stopped coming up with ideas for her needle.

That summer of 1972, bright yellows and rich prints had been left from a series of school outfits she'd made for cousins the previous fall. The quilt made from them was connected to family, like so much I experienced that summer. Later in my stay, I helped one of my cousins with the family genealogy, bringing many of the stories my grandmother had told me full circle as I examined birth, marriage, and death records, and endless newspaper reports.

That quilt—and that summer—grounded me and gave me roots as nothing else could. It went with me when I returned home, and was one of the quilts I chose when I set up my own first home after college.

Sometimes dismissing the past happens carelessly, as if it's unconnected to what and who we are. The Bible, however, instructs us to examine our roots, to talk to those who came before us. The heritage of our faith and family lives in those around us. Just listening to them can bring treasures more valuable than gold.

PRAYER STARTER

- - - - - - - - - - - - - -

Father, learning from those who came before us is a vital part of our spiritual journey. Help us lift them up with respect and love. Amen.

Starting a New Home

TULIP

- -

You who are young, be happy while you are young,
and let your heart give you joy in the days of your youth.
Follow the ways of your heart and whatever your eyes see.

Ecclesiastes 11:9

- -

It was the biggest box in the substantial stack of presents on the white-and-green-decorated table. Even though I already knew what was in it, I couldn't wait to strip off the bright wrapping paper and show the crowd at my wedding shower the gift tucked inside.

Mother and Grandmother Ila had worked for months, piecing and stitching the Tulip quilt. I'd picked the pattern and the multiple colors so it would go with any décor my new husband and I picked for our bedroom. The bright reds, blues, purples, and soft greens were among my favorite colors. The women at the shower oohed and aahed as I hoped they would, appreciating the fine needlework. I hugged the quilt, and I couldn't wait to get it into my new home, where it matched nothing.

Our new home wound up being primarily orange and brown, and the vivid Tulip quilt clashed. I insisted it be used on the bed for a while, under the spread, but it always wound up on the floor, crumpled and tripped over. After a few weeks, I rolled my beloved Tulip and stored it away in the closet. The disappointment stung, but I got over it.

I had too much going on as a newlywed to worry much about one quilt. We were young and embraced all that life could offer.

I never forgot it, however, and the Tulip went with me through a few moves and décor changes, as well as a few life changes. Eleven years later, I was single again, and the Tulip reemerged, keeping me warm and winter cozy. With all that had happened over those eleven years—good and bad—I'd lost the need for everything in my life to be color coordinated. Comfortable nostalgia took the place of appearance, and the quilt wound up being draped over a worn but snug yellow couch.

Sometimes we want something so much, we try to force it to happen, especially when we're young. We want our own way, no matter what stands against us. But if we, as the writer of Ecclesiastes advises, follow the way of our heart, of what we see in front of us, we'll learn to embrace life's joys. If something we want was meant to be, it'll circle around again. If not, God will show us new paths for joy.

PRAYER STARTER

- - - - - - - - - - - - - -

Father, help us see the true happiness that lies in front of us. Relieve us of ego-driven desires and show us Your path for our lives. Amen.

A Symbol of Hope

OHIO STAR

- - - - - - - - - - - - - - - - - - - -

Surely He has borne our griefs
And carried our sorrows.

Isaiah 53:4 NKJV

- - - - - - - - - - - - - - - - - - - -

In 1939, changes around the world spoke of a new era. The World's Fair opened in New York, and the film versions of *Gone with the Wind* and *The Wizard of Oz* premiered. Ted Williams hit his first home run, and the *Dixie Clipper* completed the first commercial flight to Europe. In some areas, signs that the Depression was easing raised hopes.

In other areas, deprivation and poverty still reigned. Prosperity took much longer to reach the rural areas, even though the federal work programs had helped improve conditions. At thirteen, my mother seldom carried to school more than a biscuit and a piece of ham for lunch. Jobs remained scarce, and thousands of families still relied primarily on what they could produce themselves. In Europe, the clouds of war expanded, culminating with Hitler's invasion of Poland in September. Jews fled persecution throughout Europe and Russia.

And in a small, struggling Alabama town, my grandmother Ila decided to quilt hope. For months, she'd scrounged and saved scraps of fabric from her factory job as well as work clothes that could no longer be repaired. A pair of pants with torn knees and a frayed rear still had strength in the thighs or calves. Sacks containing feed or flour were bleached and stitched together to make the back. Handpicked cotton bolls were carded free of seeds and tucked away for the batting.

She chose the Ohio Star pattern because it reminded her of the Star of Bethlehem. Grandmother Ila had an unshakable conviction that God and His Son would get them through whatever the economy dropped on them. She never stopped believing that conditions would improve, but even if they didn't, her family would be sustained by what God would provide.

It's a faith I can only aspire to. I've been through more than a few tough seasons, but not once did I have to grow my own food or make do without the basics. Grandmother Ila did, yet her faith did not waver. Sometimes I'm asked why I so treasure a quilt that's faded and lumpy. It's because in my family, the Ohio Star is more than a quilt. It's a symbol of hope.

PRAYER STARTER
- - - - - - - - - - - - -

Lord, we are eternally grateful for that "cloud of witnesses" that has gone before us, leaving behind their faith and their hope. Help us have as sound a faith and as great a hope. Amen.

Offhand Comments

CHURN DASH

- -

Do not say, "Why were the old days better than these?"
~~For it is not wise to ask such questions.~~
Wisdom, like an inheritance, is a good thing
and benefits those who see the sun.

Ecclesiastes 7:10–11

- -

Sometimes I see my friends cringe when I start a sentence with "My mother used to say . . ." or "Daddy used to . . ." I understand completely. Although they respect my parents, I quote something they said or did *a lot*. Mother had sayings that held great wisdom, whereas my dad had traveled and done a lot, especially when he was young. He was, for instance, the first one to tell me not to eat ice cream and then get on a roller coaster. He also taught me useful things like how to use a CB radio and change a tire.

And Daddy was more nostalgic about "the good ol' days" than Mother was, especially after work transferred him out of his beloved Alabama. This might be why Daddy's favorite quilt, out of all the ones Mother created, was the Churn Dash, with its vibrant blues, reds, and yellows. He loved the colors, but also the reminder of simpler times. His memories of those times were softer and dreamier, where Mother remembered hard work, hot kitchens, and wringer washers that would snatch young girls' fingers into danger. She had fond memories, yes, but no desire to go back in time.

The only reason we know this quilt was his favorite is an offhand comment he made when she was airing out some of her quilts, something she did several times a year. He pointed at the blue one with his pipe and said, "That one. That's the one I like best." It was part of a longer conversation about quilts and childhood memories, but Mother latched on to it, later mentioning it to me in a similarly casual manner.

But the impact it had on me wasn't casual. She told me this shortly after my dad had died, when all our memories of him were fresh and raw. My father and I loved each other dearly, but he didn't always understand me or my choices in life. He felt that we would have been closer if he hadn't take us out of Alabama, and he regretted that he couldn't help me more, especially after my divorce. Finally, we had a heartfelt conversation about all this, one of pure honesty, that left both of us in tears. Our goal? To make sure neither of us left any concern unsaid. It cleared the air between us, but it didn't make his death a few months later any easier.

So any small gift he handed me was a treasure.

"Can I have the Churn Dash?" I asked my mother a few weeks after his funeral. The question startled her, but she rolled it up, slipped it into a pillowcase, and handed it to me as I left for home. Unlike the quilts that are stored and pampered, this one gets used on my bed every winter because an offhand comment turned it into something precious.

We hear often—and my mother used to repeat this a lot—that children absorb everything they hear, even when they pretend otherwise. So do all our loved ones. A kind word—or an angry one—carries a lot of weight. Nothing that needs to be said should remain unsaid. Words used wisely, even more than money—or quilts—are the inheritance we pass to those around us.

PRAYER STARTER

- - - - - - - - - - - - - -

Lord, please pass to me Your wisdom
so that my words will lift others up,
not tear them down. Let others see
Your inheritance in me. Amen.

That Which Does Not Fade

TWENTY-FIVE PATCH

- -

Let us know; let us press on to know the LORD;
his going out is sure as the dawn; he will come to us as
the showers, as the spring rains that water the earth.

Hosea 6:3 ESV

- -

Sarah Jane Rickles Battles lived her entire life in St. Clair County, Alabama, where she died in 1911. Anyone who knew her—and knew the sound of her voice, the temper of her demeanor, the wisdom in her words—is also gone. The quilt she left behind, however, stands as a devout testimony to her attention to detail, her hard work, and her sound faith.

According to the tag my mother stitched to the back of the quilt, Sarah Jane "spun the thread, wove the cloth" for the back of it. The colors on the front appear to be from shirt and dress material of the period, which means Sarah

Jane wasted nothing. The tag also points out that, as with many of the quilts of this period, the cotton batting was handpicked and hand-carded. The stitches are tiny, the quilting patterns intricate and precise, made with a thick thread that has darkened with age.

But in one block of patches, amidst the pale reds and browns, are three bright blue squares. Unlike the other colors, they haven't faded because they are indigo, one of the few dyes that never loses its brilliance. But why are they there? They don't belong, standing out like a flower in a snowbank. In the midst of the excellent work Sarah Jane put into this quilt, they look like a mistake, which seems unlikely given the craft of the quilt.

The answer is that only God is without error. Some quilters of that period, as many Amish do today, intentionally built flaws into their quilts, recognition that perfection belongs only to the Lord. In Sarah Jane's case, she probably didn't realize that in choosing the indigo squares, she picked the one "flaw" that never fades.

In passing down this imperfection, my great-great grandmother inadvertently reminded all who came after her how impermeable and unchanging is God's true love for us. It is a love that will come to us no matter what, showering us "as the spring rains," always refreshing and new.

PRAYER STARTER

- - - - - - - - - - - - -

Lord, Your love never fails, never weakens, never fades. Help us remember Your goodness in times of feast as well as famine. Amen.

Comforting the Sick

BLEEDING HEARTS

- -

Blessed be God, even the Father of our Lord Jesus Christ,
the Father of mercies, and the God of all comfort;
Who comforteth us in all our tribulation, that we may be
able to comfort them which are in any trouble,
by the comfort wherewith we ourselves are comforted of God.

2 Corinthians 1:3–4 KJV

- -

The red and white quilt, worn soft with use and age, is the quilt of my childhood.

Completed in 1940 by my grandmother Ila, it had been made for mattresses not quite as wide as modern beds. That made it perfect for couches and floor pallets, blanket forts and rocking chairs in front of the fire. Mother carried it with her when she got married and when her young family left for a new town. A stay-at-home mom, she wanted sick kids close at hand, so she'd pile us up on the den couch with the Bleeding Hearts quilt and set up a TV tray with crackers and ginger ale. When fever and chills set me or my brother to shivering, it was this quilt she wrapped around us to tuck us in tightly.

Then, as Mother started quilting again and our grandmothers visited more, newer quilts took over. Soft but lumpy cotton battings gave way to smooth rolls of filler. The comfy red and white Bleeding Hearts quilt was relegated to padding for furniture moves or a spare when guests stayed over. Otherwise, it was tucked into a closet out of the way. But it didn't languish there long.

It reappeared when my parents retired and moved back to Alabama. Its soft warmth and red hearts made a perfect drape for one of their sofas.
When my daughter was born, the now velvety cotton made it ideal for her tender skin. Throughout the years, it has remained our steadfast comforter, through good times and bad.

We all need such steadfastness in our lives, whether it's the love of those close, a familiar quilt, or the loyalty of friends. They bolster us, providing the emotional support we crave. None, however, is as unwavering as the guidance, wisdom, and strength we receive from God. No matter what our trials, His comfort will be with us always.

PRAYER STARTER

- - - - - - - - - - - - - -

Father, forgive us when we cling more to earthly comforts than to Your unchanging consolation. Help us remember that You never let us down. Amen.

Center of the Home

PUZZLE

- -

Do not neglect to show hospitality to strangers,
for thereby some have entertained angels unawares.

Hebrews 13:2 ESV

- -

"The kitchen table is the heart of your home. Make it warm and inviting, and friends will linger and come back." Mother told me that enough that it was embroidered on my brain, and she usually followed it with the verse from Hebrews. She believed in "angels unawares" more than anyone I ever met, and she raised us with firm ideas about kindness and hospitality.

While money never came to us in abundance, Mother worked hard to make sure that her home remained clean, and she decorated the table with fruit that filled the air with a welcoming sweetness. Other smells lingered as well: cinnamon, honey, and bread. My friends loved visiting, and she welcomed them always. Any bad mood was set aside once company arrived.

Quilts, which draped the den couch and rockers, added to the reception. Quilted place mats and a runner made the kitchen table seem like an extension of the den. I remember many hours gathered around that table, sometimes just family, sometimes friends. We enjoyed each other's company, and conversation usually lasted long past the time the plates were cleaned and the cookies devoured.

But Mother entertained more than family and friends. I'd also come home from school on occasion to see a complete stranger nursing a cup of coffee and slice of pie. It might be the new preacher, or a guy who'd been working

in the yard next door who looked too hot. Mother had grown up on a farm, in a time when manual laborers would walk from town to town looking for work. Her own mother, my grandmother Ila, would offer up well water and a ham biscuit to all comers. My mother continued this tradition with a simple philosophy: "You never know what that other fellow's story may be."

It's an ideal that's served me well. While the world has changed, and opening your front door to strangers is no longer a good idea, having an open home and heart has allowed me to welcome all sorts of friends. Many have repaid me with love, help, prayers, and support, sometimes when I needed it most and expected it least.

In many ways, we all become "angels unawares" when we love people, for we show them the love God has filled our hearts and souls with to overflowing.

PRAYER STARTER

- - - - - - - - - - -

Lord, help us embrace Your children,
holding them close. We can't awlays know their
stories; help us know their hearts. Amen.

Brighter Colors

DUTCH ROSE

- -

And all the women that were wise hearted did spin
with their hands, and brought that which
they had spun, both of blue, and of purple,
and of scarlet, and of fine linen.

Exodus 35:25 KJV

- -

My grandmother Ila lived in a rather drab world for many years. My grandfather farmed the fields surrounding the house, and in spring and summer, dust covered furniture and floors alike. In a house without air-conditioning, open windows were a necessity, but shades were kept low to cut down on the heat. Muted colors decorated the walls, and even her dresses were a modest gray or deep blue gingham.

But make no mistake, my grandmother loved bright colors. They inched their way into her life in flowers that dotted the yard and the car-sized hydrangea bushes next to the house. And, of course, in her quilts. Brilliant yellows and reds found themselves patched up next to rich greens and blues. She liked pairing up various hues of the same shade, playing light and dark against each other.

After she moved in with my parents, and without the responsibilities of home and garden, her quilts grew in

intricacy, and the puzzle of putting the pieces together thrilled her. One weekend I came home from college to find her carefully pinning together a purple Dutch Rose. "That's bright," I said. "Gorgeous purple."

"God likes purple," she muttered through a mouthful of pins. I thought she was joking until she spoke at dinner that night about the fine linens in the temple, of the rich colors the women had brought.

I told her that purple was traditionally the color of royalty, a fact that didn't faze her at all. She just nodded. "We should wear more. After all, we're God's children." She looked straight at me. "Royalty. We should act as such. Treat each other as such."

Then she went back to work on a purple quilt as fine as any monarch's cape.

PRAYER STARTER

- - - - - - - - - - - - - -

Father, we are indeed Your children,
heirs to Your kingdom. Help us remember
that so that we behave in a manner
worthy of Your name. Amen.

Family Ties

SAMPLER

- -

Train up a child in the way he should go:
and when he is old, he will not depart from it.

Proverbs 22:6 KJV

- -

I didn't know for many years that my mother owned this quilt. She kept it tucked away in her cedar chest, rolled and carefully wrapped in a clean muslin cloth. Few things made it into her cedar chest, but this one was there along with one of my infant dresses, Daddy's military discharge, and a hand-tatted dress she had worn as a toddler.

Just as an embroidery sampler is meant to teach the different types of stitches, a sampler quilt demonstrates a new quilter's ability to handle different patterns. The result is an explosion of color and a riot of some of the most well-known blocks all crammed into one comfy spread. The pinks, blues, purples, and golden yellows of this quilt date at least to the 1940s, as does the lumpy cotton batting.

Bow ties snuggle up against flying geese, nine-patches, diamonds, and bars.

It is clearly a student's quilt. The patterns are neat but don't always match up as they should. The stitch length varies widely, and what should be straight rows—and thus easy to quilt—are not. But despite its flaws, this is a quilt that's been used and loved. Some of the frayed patches have given way, letting small cotton tufts stick out around the quilting. A slight discoloration around the edges speaks of generations of hands that have tugged it a little higher on the bed, arms that have cuddled beneath its warmth.

It belonged to a family of quilters, and this was the training ground. All of the quilts that followed were better made, perhaps were even longer lasting. But this is where those skills were honed.

This is a truth we should remember when we teach those around us, whether we are imparting our faith, our skills, or our love. What people learn as children seems to cling more tightly than what they learn when they get older.

I know my mother believed this with all her heart, as she repeated it constantly during my teenage wanderings. My rebellion made her heart ache, but she truly believed that having raised me in the church, I would one day return.

My mother—and the writer of Proverbs—knew what they were talking about.

PRAYER STARTER

Father, helps us gently guide the young minds around us toward You. As we show them Your loving ways, may they never stray far from Your wise path. Amen.

A Distant Vision

CATHEDRAL WINDOW

- -

Commit your work to the LORD,
and your plans will be established.

Proverbs 16:3 ESV

- -

My grandmother Ila's health began to fail as she approached eighty. As sometimes happens, the changes appeared to come on suddenly, with increasing weakness and loss of weight. She'd never been a robust woman—she'd been exceptionally thin her entire life—but she'd always had good health. But now we had to recognize she wouldn't be around for many more years.

Yet my grandmother yearned to make one more quilt— her dream quilt, actually. One she'd wanted to do for years but had dared not take on during the years my grandfather had been sick with his final illness. Completing a Cathedral Window quilt is a daunting task. It's a completely different technique from a standard patchwork, requiring hundreds of tiny color patches and hour upon hour of delicate and intricate hand stitching of the squares. The stitches needed to tuck the bits of color in the white circles must be uniform or the quilt will look uneven.

This is an undertaking that younger, healthier women would find intimidating, yet my grandmother dove into the project with gusto. Once when Mother commented that she might not complete it before she died, my grandmother replied stoically, "That's in God's hands. If He wants it finished, I'll live long enough to finish it."

Her statement dropped a mustard seed in front of all of our family, and her desire to finish this quilt instilled in both my brother and me a drive to "not wait" to pursue something we wanted to achieve. My grandmother's work on this quilt changed all of us.

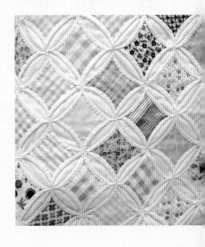

Grandmother Ila finished the quilt. Then she decided she wanted to make it big enough for a bedspread, so she went back and added two more rows. God saw her through it all. And more. She not only lived to complete the hardest quilt she'd attempted, she went on to quilt more, surviving the Cathedral Window by more than a decade. But it wasn't the reality of her longevity that made the quilt special to our family; it was the faith with which she stepped out into the unknown that inspired us all.

PRAYER STARTER

- - - - - - - - - - - -

Lord, when we set our eyes on You first, we can do anything. Help us remember this first, and best, step toward achieving any goal. Amen.

Staying True

RIBBON

- -

Let not mercy and truth forsake you;
Bind them around your neck,
Write them on the tablet of your heart.

Proverbs 3:3 NKJV

- -

This quilt is a mystery. Mother never tagged it because she had no idea who made it or how old it was. The fabric places it in the 1940s, but beyond that, little information about it exists.

Still, there are telltale signs that reveal a great deal about it. It was carefully pieced and quilted, with admirable precision. It has a distinct patterned binding that's not used anywhere else in the quilt, which sets it apart from the other quilts I have from that same period. The backing is definitely made from bleached feedsacks, with a cotton batting. There are almost no signs of wear. No discoloring around the edges from ages of oily hands. No frayed corners or foxed edges. No embedded folds or creases. No pulled threads, although there are a few squares that have puckered, mostly likely after being washed. But this quilt has been treasured and seldom used.

The pattern is one that's been called a number of things—a ribbon pattern or an Indian hatchet, among others—but with no word on the creator, there's no way of knowing for sure what pattern she intended. My mother thought that my grandmother Ila probably made it, as the top is machine-stitched, and the tension and length of the stitches bear a close resemblance to some of the professional work Grandmother Ila did when she worked in a factory.

The quilt became special to my mother, however, because she found it amidst the quilts left behind when my grandmother died. Even though Grandmother Ila had lived with us, Mother gave her as much privacy as she could, so she wasn't familiar with every-

thing my grandmother had tucked away. The first time Mother pulled it out of the closet and spread it across a bed, she stared at it a few moments, then muttered, "That ribbon is like the blood of Christ. It runs through everything and affects everything it touches."

Mother wasn't a woman given to idealistic notions or strong metaphors. So for her to say such a thing indicated just how much she missed her mom and their long chats about God, faith, and the afterlife. I am, however, given to drawing connections when strong memories are involved, and I miss both of these women every day. So to me, the actual pattern of this quilt is irrelevant. It is, instead, a symbol of the blood of Christ and how it runs through all of us, connecting all of God's children into one family.

PRAYER STARTER

_Lord, we are Your children in one family.
Guide us toward understanding and
acceptance of each other, as Your Son
connects us all. Amen._

Changing Courses

BALTIMORE APPLIQUÉ

- -

Don't be anxious about anything; rather,
bring up all of your requests to God in your prayers
and petitions, along with giving thanks.
Then the peace of God that exceeds all understanding
will keep your hearts and minds safe in Christ Jesus.

Philippians 4:6–7 CEB

- -

Mother was nervous. She'd been quilting for many years, and she'd felt her creativity needed a boost. She wanted to try something new, a quilt that would test her mettle. Yet failure loomed in her mind. Yes, she could always set it aside and start over. But she and Daddy lived on a limited income, and Mother had always been a frugal woman. The idea of wasting that much cloth intimidated her.

Appliqué. Such a simple word to create such anxiety. But the quilt Mother chose to tackle was anything but simple: a basket quilt, an appliqué pattern based on quilts that originated in Baltimore in the 1840s. With a pattern that covered an entire quilt space instead of one block, and required the precision of a needle-turning technique to hide the stitches, Mother stepped into completely unknown territory. Ever the careful crafter, she measured, pinned, measured again. She studied the pattern until she had it memorized. She'd stand at the end of the bed and stare at the pinned map of fabric until she had convinced herself she could do this. Finally, as she did with most things, she prayed over it.

Mother believed in the power of prayer with a ferocity I've known in few other people. "Have you talked to God

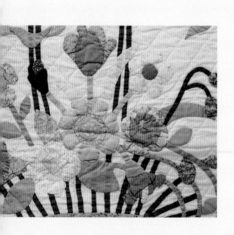

about it?" was a frequent topic of our conversations. She prayed about both of her kids, just as many moms do, and that didn't stop just because we grew up and moved away. I once fussed at her, "Don't worry about me. I'm good."

She scolded back, "I don't worry about you. That does no good. I turned you over to God a long time ago. Doesn't mean I don't care about what happens to you, though." Mother encouraged me to develop my own pattern of prayer and trust—especially when attempting something new—which has served me well over the years. We both believed that God answered all prayers, although we didn't always like the responses.

So the fact that she would pray over her quilt surprised me not at all. Afterward, she took a deep breath and picked up the scissors.

With her house and volunteer work, she didn't have a lot of time to spend on the Baltimore quilt, but it slowly took shape. She made it king-sized, so she could use it as a bedspread, and it topped my parents' bed for many years, a gorgeous testimony to her care and her belief in trusting God, no matter what she had to tackle.

PRAYER STARTER

Lord, You love us and guide us in new endeavors
as well as our everyday lives. Help us remember
to trust You in all things. Amen.

The Parts Come Together

ROSETTE BASKET

- -

Two are better than one; because they have
a good reward for their labour. For if they fall,
the one will lift up his fellow: but woe to him that is alone
when he falleth; for he hath not another to help him up.
Again, if two lie together, then they have heat:
but how can one be warm alone?
And if one prevail against him, two shall withstand him;
and a threefold cord is not quickly broken.

Ecclesiastes 4:9–12 KJV

- -

Thy look like yo-yos." I plucked a few of the colorful circlets out of the basket next to Mother's chair. The dark greens, bright pinks, and random polka dots seemed unconnected to each other, despite the common puckered circle in the middle.

"Some people call them that," Mother responded. "Or rosettes. I prefer rosettes. It's prettier." When I asked what they were for, she just smiled. "Wait and see."

It became her after-supper treat, to sit and create mounds of the little rounds. A basket full, stitched and dropped in as if they were beans being snapped or peas shelled. Then, finally, they began showing up on pillows and centerpieces, coming together in mosaics that dotted the house with happy colors. The culmination was a wall hanging on which dozens of rosettes formed a delightful basket.

The unmatched and unrelated bits came together to form a new creation. "Quilts are so often like a puzzle of companion colors," Mother explained. "I love that all these mismatched scraps come together to make something new. The many into a whole."

After she completed the basket hanging, Mother continued to work on major quilt projects, many of which challenged her creativity and her skills. But rosettes continued to be her creative "snack," a quick bit of sewing she could do after the day's chores had been completed. And when she died, I found a box of unused rosettes, just waiting to be made into something special.

In many ways, the wide variety of Jesus' followers are like Mother's rosettes. We are made up of different temperaments, colors, interests, backgrounds. But we all come together as one church, one body under one God. We are lovely as individuals, but when we join together, we can be spectacular.

PRAYER STARTER

Father God, You unite us. You make us into Your church through the sacrifice of Your Son. May we always remember that love of You is what stitches us together. Amen.

Different Shades of One Color

DIAMOND COMPASS

- -

Live in harmony with one another.

Romans 12:16

- -

Most of Grandmother Ila's quilts were starbursts of coordinated colors. Brash yellows blended with a red and yellow print. Purples and reds bumped against companion blues and pinks. So when she chose a gentle variety of greens for her new quilt, Mother and I wanted to know why.

She just shrugged. "It seems right." She said the same thing about the pattern she'd chosen, a variation of a compass pattern.

Grandmother Ila had turned seventy-seven that past January. She'd been living with my parents less than two years, and this was the second quilt she'd started. In many ways, she was still finding her place after being uprooted from her Alabama home. Away from friends, family, and church, she struggled with loneliness, and each day she became more dependent on my mom for company.

At the same time, my mother's routine clashed with what Grandmother Ila was used to. They danced around each other in the kitchen, in the laundry room. Mother was usually a whirling dervish when she cleaned or cooked. My grandmother moved slower, more deliberately, as she always had. They tried to live in harmony, but they were often on each other's nerves as they tried to deal with the new normal. Even after two years, neither had compromised much.

Grandmother Ila had been the oldest girl of eight children, and had been only eleven when her mother died in childbirth. She'd become a mother to her siblings, and her life had never been easy . . . or lonely. Now she faced a time when nothing was required of her and few of the people she loved were around. She needed a new direction.

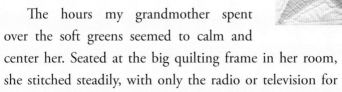

The hours my grandmother spent over the soft greens seemed to calm and center her. Seated at the big quilting frame in her room, she stitched steadily, with only the radio or television for company. Slowly she relaxed, adjusting to yet another new routine, this one centered around a quilt.

One day I came home to find my mother and grandmother both quilting and chatting. Slowly they found a way to harmony. My mother lived almost thirty years longer than her mom, and she once told me she missed her every day.

Scripture tells us to live in harmony, to appreciate other people and their gifts, to not turn anyone away just because you don't understand them. It's not always easy, but there's always a path, if we just pay attention.

PRAYER STARTER

- - - - - - - - - - - - -

Lord, help us look around and see other believers
as equals, fellow members of Your family.
Guide us into harmony with them. Amen.

Joy in the Making

HEARTS IN BLOOM

---

*But the fruit of the Spirit is love, joy, peace,
longsuffering, gentleness, goodness, faith.*

Galatians 5:22 KJV

When Daddy had a heart attack in 1990, Mother set about changing their lifestyle, especially how they ate. Southern home cooking isn't always good for the heart. And Daddy had a hard time accepting her new recipes at first. Mother never gave up researching new ways to turn her traditional food into heart-wise fare. They both started walking up to three miles a day, in addition to tending the one-acre garden they put in every year.

But when cancer settled in on Daddy in 1995, Mother made him her focus, with endless trips to the doctor and hospital. She researched his treatments and tried to keep him from overdoing it, which in itself was a full-time task. Daddy wasn't much for sitting idle. Mother's solution-prone soul wanted to make everything right again, and she chafed that all their efforts were to no avail. With little warning, Daddy had a bad reaction to the treatments. He fell ill one afternoon in May 1996, pneumonia set in, and he had no resistance. Within twenty-four hours he was gone.

After everything was over, Mother fought hard to rebuild her life. Loneliness became a ragged-toothed enemy, and she volunteered at the library, then the hospital. She changed to a larger, more active church and sought out their activities for seniors.

The local quilters' guild, which she'd been a member of for a while, gathered around her with friendship and support. And, of course, there were her quilts.

Just over a year after Daddy's death, she began work on a Hearts in Bloom quilt. The serene roses, blues, and greens quieted her spirit, she said, and the intricate quilting occupied her mind. She edged the elements of each block, but around them added stitching in the patterns of leaves and hearts. During this hard period of transition, I'd ask her how she was doing, and Mother would usually respond, "Quilting and praying."

Adjusting to the loss of a loved one is always difficult, a time of suffering as well as recovery. Calling on her love and trust in God, Mother bore it with faith and honor, remembering her love for my father even as she redirected her life toward a place of joy with prayer . . . and quilts.

PRAYER STARTER

*Lord, help us call on the fruits of the Spirit
in our own lives to help those around us.
Guide us toward those who are lonely or lost,
and let them see Your love in
and through us. Amen.*

Pink Is the Color

AMISH DIAMOND

Lo, children are an heritage of the LORD:
and the fruit of the womb is his reward.

Psalm 127:3 KJV

I've never been a patient person. So no one was surprised when it turned out my daughter, Rachel, wasn't either. She showed up early, after only six months of pregnancy. Weighing in at just over two pounds, Rachel's premature arrival meant weeks of hospitalization, tests . . . and even more waiting, this time to see what difficulties she might have. Nine more months passed before my husband and I found out exactly what her disabilities would be.

The verdict wasn't kind. Severe cerebral palsy. Seizures. Brain trauma. Rachel, we were told, would never walk, talk, or care for herself. She'd have a shortened life expectancy. We received the information with numbness, shock. We took Rachel home to a house full of useless toys and games, all given in joy by loving friends and relatives. While we tried to adjust to this sea change in our lives, we questioned everything we believed. If children are to be a reward from God, what had we done? Who were we?

With her own sense of loss still settling in, Mother turned to what she knew best: prayers and quilting. While

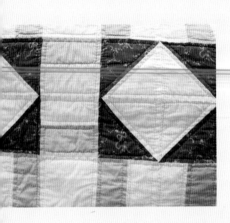

Rachel would never know the joy of mobiles, blocks, or tricycles, Mother knew she would experience lots of love and cuddling. Asking God for wisdom, Mother put her needle to work.

The blue triangles, pink bars, and white diamonds became a soft, warm comforter for Rachel's bed, a reminder that I had Mother and Daddy's support for whatever trials were to come.

And come they did. Pneumonia, more times than I can count. Grand mal seizures. Surgery. But along with the trials came great wonder: A laugh that can warm a roomful of people. A sweetness beyond compare. A love of music that keeps her content, and a fondness for girly ribbons and dresses. And a stubbornness that reminds us she is still all girl.

I was transformed by this child. I would not be the person I am without her. I came to see that the rewards she brought from God were not that much different from those from other children. While she is unlike those kids, she is my beautiful reward. My mother could not have prayed for anything better.

PRAYER STARTER

Father, all Your children are gifts, and those
You give to us are indeed rewards,
no matter what they are like. Guide us
as we raise them up in Your love. Amen.

Strength in the Gathering

FRIENDSHIP

- -

And let us consider one another in order to stir up love and good works, not forsaking the assembling of ourselves together, as is the manner of some, but exhorting one another.

Hebrews 10:24–25 *NKJV*

- -

When Mother began quilting again in the 1970s, we lived in Tennessee, and her main support in her craft was my grandmother, who lived with us from 1977 to 1985. Because of Mother's other obligations, quilts took a long time to complete. When my father retired and they returned to Alabama, however, Mother discovered the quilters' guild in Hartselle. With their support and encouragement, her skills and production skyrocketed, and she dove headfirst into books and magazines, embracing new patterns and methods like a kid at play.

One of the activities of the guild especially tickled her: friendship quilts. Fabric bought by the guild would be divvied up to each member, who would return the next week with her own unique square. The pieced tops were given to the local senior center for the quilting.

Despite the many varying patterns in the squares, the resulting pieced tops were gorgeous, with the same colors reflecting the interests and skills of each guild member. Mother always claimed that she'd learned a great deal from each one by examining the other quilters' techniques and pattern choices. Friendship quilts challenged her, and the other members, to be better at their craft. Their individual talents, when drawn together, strengthened each other and produced an heirloom in the process. This community project, however, bonded the women in other ways as well. They were all believers, and working on a common quilt stimulated conversation, provided a shared experience, and deepened friendships and faith. In some ways, the guild reminded Mother of her Sunday school classes.

Throughout my life, Mother always encouraged me to join a church. With a church family, she insisted, you're never alone. As a single mother, I found this to be profoundly true; my church carried me through more than a few times of crisis. What Mother found in her quilters' guild and Sunday school classes, I found in church friends who never let me fall, no matter how hard life turned out. The words of Hebrews are as true today as it was when those words were written. When we come together as a community, we are stronger and more supportive than we can be alone.

PRAYER STARTER

- - - - - - - - - - - - -

Father, show me how to lift up those around me,
encouraging them in their good works
and a strong faith. Amen.

Separation from Family

OCEAN WAVES

- -

It gave me great joy when some believers came and testified about your faithfulness to the truth, telling how you continue to walk in it. I have no greater joy than to hear that my children are walking in the truth.

3 John 3–4

- -

Mother preferred to quilt and pray rather than worry, which is one reason she made so many quilts after my brother and I left home. Neither of us strayed that far while we still lived under the same roof as Mother and Daddy, although we gave them more than a bit of grief. We saved our truly rebellious times for those years after eighteen, when we were off spreading our wings. We definitely gave Mother plenty to pray about.

Mother told me, years later, that she prayed most about my lack of faith. I had left the church in my late teens, and in my twenties I explored a whole range of different beliefs, including Wicca. While she firmly believed that a child raised in Christianity would eventually return to it, she found herself uncomfortable with my days of exploration. She said she had to believe God would always win, and prayed for my protection and those of my friends.

Those prayers worked, as I found myself lured back to the church in my thirties. I still had a lot of doubts, but God placed me in a place where I could question freely and have those concerns answered by knowledgeable men and women with strong foundations of faith. At one point, I taped the words from Mark 9:24 on my phone, praying it every day: "I do believe; help me overcome my unbelief!" Eventually, I didn't require the daily reminder.

One day, as Mother and I discussed that passage in Scripture and how much it meant to me, she paused and told me I was her "prodigal come home to roost."

She quilted this with me in mind. The pattern, with its flying geese triangles flowing in crisscrossed waves, reminded her of the winding nature of my life's course. "You couldn't take a straight line from here to there if you tried. You love to wander too much."

No matter how often or how far I strayed, I always found my way home. Spiritually, as well as physically.

As parents, sometimes our instinct is to hold our children close, to protect them from the perils of the world. But we can't always do that; children will always wander. Instead, Scripture shows us how to give them the foundation they need to explore, and the guidance for them to return home when they are ready.

PRAYER STARTER

Father, Your Word is filled with guidance and wisdom for parents and children alike. Help us guide those in our care along Your path for our lives. Amen.

A Lap of Love

SQUARES IN SQUARES

- -

I have shown you in every way, by laboring like this,
that you must support the weak.
And remember the words of the Lord Jesus, that He said,
"It is more blessed to give than to receive."

Acts 20:35 NKJV

- -

Some quilts are treasures, meant to be coddled and preserved. Mother made a number of these, with weeks, sometimes months, spent on meticulous choices of patterns and fabrics, triple measurements, and cautious cutting. Cloth turned into fine art through care, imagination, and craft.

Others are simple, more functional than artful.

Mother went through a period when she wanted desperately to help me with my daughter, Rachel, whose disabilities left those around us uncertain, even scared, about how to deal with her. Normal childhood gifts of toys and games were useless. Rachel loved music, but her pickiness made her impossible to buy for. So Mother turned to the practical. Quilted and overstuffed cushions for the cane-bottom rocker where Rachel and I spent so much time. Homemade bedsheets custom-sized to fit her crib and various floor pallets. Tiny, sculpted pillows for her head. And an infinite number of throws in various sizes and weights. Throws for laps, couches, beds, and Rachel's wheelchair. Mother wanted to make sure she never got cold.

To be honest, not all of them were useful. A hot child with her own internal furnace, Rachel seldom needed more than a onesie to be comfortable. When I held her, together we could generate enough heat to warm a small room. Many of Mother's productions wound up being draped over the back of chairs, spread across tables, or tossed in a heap at the end of the couch. Even though I didn't use them often, I wanted all these tumbles of color close at hand.

They were made with love and a desire to be close to us when she couldn't be.

Now that Rachel is in her twenties, the smaller pieces no longer fit her bed or her wheelchair. Some have disappeared over time, left at school or day care, forgotten on a bus or in a hotel room. Spills and other childhood accidents meant some had to be destroyed. A few survived, like the black and red lap quilt, which I keep draped over the back of my home office recliner. It's light but warm, and is a comfortable reminder that—as Scripture tells us—when we do anything out of pure love, some element of that remains, no matter how much time passes.

PRAYER STARTER

Lord, as Your children, love should be our first law, as You commanded. May all we do reflect Your love for us and our love for others. Amen.

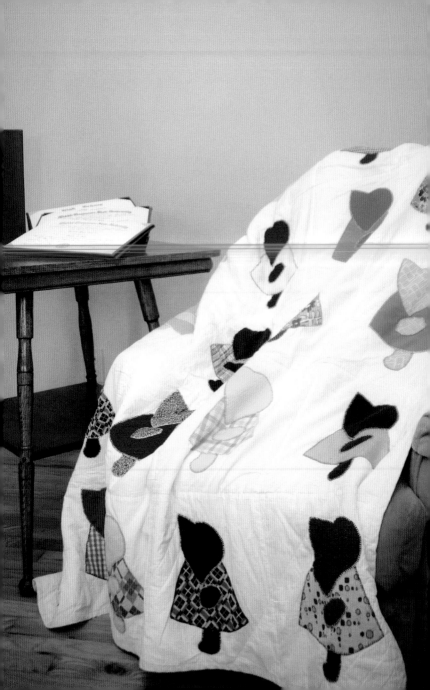

Repairing the Damage

DUTCH DOLL

Even a child is known by his doings,
whether his work be pure, and whether it be right.

Proverbs 20:11 *KJV*

For the most part, I was what most folks would call a "good kid." I had a lot of respect for my parents, and as a teenager, I never strayed too far from the spiritual path they wanted me to follow. My first year in college changed all that, however.

In spreading my wings, I made a few serious missteps. My best friend and I craved adventure and sought it out in some dangerous ways—one of my excursions ended with a broken ankle. Another left my car in a ditch, while another had us up on a mountaintop, standing around a fire as the Wiccans with us "raised a cone of power." Alcohol wedged its way into my world, and I even took one history exam in a less than sober state. Yet, in hindsight, I can see the times God worked in my life to protect me from serious harm.

All of this took a toll on my relationship with my mother, however. We drifted apart, especially as some of my friends began to concern her. Her warnings made me defensive and distant. She wanted me in a church, wanted to help me. I wanted to be left alone to find my own way.

Then two things happened at the same time, which I later saw as God's timing. I ripped my Dutch Doll quilt just before returning home at the end of my freshman year. Then I came down with mononucleosis, which left me

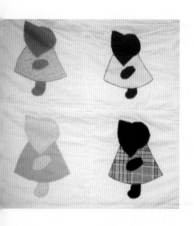

fatigued and aimless. Unable to work my summer job, I found myself sitting at home, too weak to even hold a paperback book. Television held no interest for me, so I wound up spending hours with my mother, just talking. It was all I could manage.

We'd settle on the couch—me with a half-dozen pillows, her with her lap quilting hoop—and she'd stitch while I'd pretend to be well. Or we'd join my dad on the front porch, watching the neighborhood as we talked. And sooner or later, everything came out—my feelings about boys, friends, and school, her concerns about my behavior. My defensiveness melted away as I realized she just wanted what was best for me. She began to understand that I had to walk a very different course than the one she'd hoped.

And I began to believe, as she did, that all of it was under God's control. Not an easy lesson to completely accept, but it's one that has bolstered me for the rest of my life.

PRAYER STARTER

Father, all our lives are in Your hands,
for which we are grateful. Help us remember that
in good times as well as bad, so that we remain
thankful for all You've done. Amen.

Stretching Ourselves

FLEUR-DE-LIS APPLIQUÉ

- -

Thy word is a lamp unto my feet,
and a light unto my path.

Psalm 119:105 *KJV*

- -

Although completing the Baltimore Basket quilt had challenged Mother, she found the idea of taking on another appliqué quilt invigorating. Since the Baltimore quilt had been pastels and lightweight, a reminder of the coming of spring, she wanted this one to be heavier, with richer colors, a harbinger of winter and the Christmas season.

As she researched possible patterns and fabrics, she came upon an article on the symbolism behind the fleur-de-lis, that abstract representation of a lily that has borne a variety of meanings over the centuries. One description that caught her eye was that the fleur-de-lis, with its three separate petals, had been used as a symbol of Christ and the Holy Trinity in religious paintings. This would be perfect for her Christmas quilt, subtle and rich. She loved the idea that it would be a reminder that Christ was her Light, the Guide of her life.

She chose a deep red, almost burgundy cloth for the fleur-de-lis appliqués and a soft cream for the background. This is the only quilt she ever made completely reversible, and she chose a complementary floral pattern for the other side. Like the Baltimore quilt, she made her fleur-de-lis king-sized so she could use it as a bedspread. From the day of its completion in 1992, she did just that, using the Baltimore in the spring and summer and the fleur-de-lis in fall and winter.

Rotating these two quilts as her bedcover became such a tradition that the year she didn't switch them out, I knew

something was wrong. By that time, she'd been in an assisted living facility for almost six years. When I asked her about it, she admitted she just didn't have the strength to move the heavy quilt off the shelf in her closet. I volunteered to do it, but she just shook her head. "You take it home. Just remember why I made it." She passed away a few weeks later.

I still have the fleur-de-lis; I remember why she made it. But

Mother was the far greater reminder that Christ is the Light on our path. She lived her belief every day, an inspiration for me to do the same.

PRAYER STARTER

- - - - - - - - - - - - -

Lord, guide us on the paths You have designed
for our lives, and show us how to live
so that we remind those around us of Your love
and presence in us. Amen.

Blending Traditions

SAMPLER

- -

Follow my example, just like I follow Christ's.
I praise you because you remember all my instructions,
and you hold on to the traditions exactly
as I handed them on to you.

1 Corinthians 11:1–2 CEB

- -

The sampler quilt finally emerged from Mother's cedar chest when she moved into an assisted living facility in 2008. With no room for the chest, the treasures inside were carefully reviewed and either sent with my brother or me, or they were tenderly packed away in a small storage box. With no room in the box for the quilt, it joined the others on her closet shelf at first. As that walk-in space became more crowded, however, the quilt landed in my hands, along with more than twenty others.

Mother made sure I knew how to care for the quilts, both new and vintage. "White, cotton gloves, or at least wash your hands thoroughly. Roll them, don't fold them.

Take them out occasionally and fluff, then reroll in a different way. Store in cloth or acid-free paper. Never, *ever* put them in plastic. Do I need to write all this down? I know you forget things."

I do forget things, especially now that I'm past fifty. But I'd heard her talk about the care of quilts enough times to have the instructions tattooed on my brain. With a reassurance that pillowcases made sufficient storage cases, I stocked up on king-sized ones so I'd have flexibility with the rolls.

When I asked her why the sampler quilt had been so special to her, she explained, "It reminds me of those last years at home, before I got married. Mama taught me how to quilt, how to stitch the blocks together. These are the basics, the traditional patterns. If you can quilt these, you can take on just about any quilt block out there." This had been the quilt on which she'd first learned those patterns. Just as many crafters treasure their first piece—I still have my first completed cross-stitch piece and the first pot I threw on a wheel—Mother never wanted that quilt too far from her hands.

Traditions sometimes take a beating in our world, as they have since the first teenagers wanted to break away from their parents' past. But Scripture—and experience—tells us that traditions exist for a reason. They form the foundation built by the experience of many generations. They hold truth and grounding for now and the future.

PRAYER STARTER

Father, thank You for the wisdom You granted believers in times gone by. They have left behind a legacy of faith and truth. Help us honor them and use those traditions to build an unshakable future. Amen.

The Need for Practicality

BLEEDING HEARTS

When it snows, she has no fear for her household;
for all of them are clothed in scarlet.
She makes coverings for her bed.

Proverbs 31:21–22

My grandmother Ila loved red. It featured prominently in many of her quilts, usually blended in among the plainer colors that had been clipped from outgrown work or school clothes. She had red handkerchiefs and dish towels for the kitchen. When I was young, she'd even sew clothes for my Barbie doll, who looked quite the hussy in her scarlet dresses and jackets.

But back in 1939, Grandmother Ila acquired some bolt ends from the factory where she worked as a seamstress. She often worked on the heavy cotton football uniforms of that era, and one team used red as the primary color. Her bosses let her keep the leftovers, and she added the scraps to her collection. Sometime in 1940, she put the finishing touches on the Bleeding Hearts quilt.

At the time my grandfather, my mother, and she lived in a wooden home outside Ashville, Alabama. They were just coming out of the Great Depression, and deprivation was still more common than not. My grandfather, a tenant farmer, drove a school bus for extra money. They lived near the gas line that ran from Birmingham to Gadsden, and for a few dollars each month, they would house the man who walked the line, inspecting it. That extra cash some-

times made the difference in whether or not they made the rent. In such a life, no one was surprised when Grandmother Ila gravitated to red.

Yet, as my mother told it, Grandmother Ila always made sure they were warm, clothed, and fed, even if there wasn't much to go around. Mother could describe with remarkable clarity the days she'd come home from school, chilled to the bone, only to be wrapped in the Bleeding Hearts quilt and stationed next to a fire until she thawed out, a cup of hot milk in her hands.

The "Proverbs 31 woman" is often held up as an ideal, although one almost impossible to attain. Yet so many of the verses in that chapter remind me of my grandmother, who strove to make sure her family had the essentials in life—food, clothes, and a warm place to come home to—but who also tried to add joy and beauty to the lives of those she loved. Sometimes the best blessings we have to offer are the ones we give out of love.

PRAYER STARTER

Lord, in the busyness of our everyday lives,
help us remember that our families
still need those basics before anything else,
along with our love. Amen.

The Mark of Creativity

MOTHER'S OWN

- -

*He has filled him with the Spirit of God, in wisdom
and understanding, in knowledge and all manner of
workmanship, to design artistic works.*

Exodus 35:31–32 NKJV

- -

Throughout Scripture there are praises to creativity, to
innovation and the design of artistic work. When God
created us in His own image, He imbued us with the same
desire to create that He has. In turn, those with a creative
spirit have either honored that gift by using it to reveal Him
to others, or they have expressed their thanks to Him.

Creativity also takes many forms, above and beyond
what we humans call the "fine arts." It's shown in what and
how we choose to teach our children and in the methods
we use to solve problems. Any scientist who's asked, "What
if?" and goes on to discover some breakthrough has demonstrated creativity. And any woman who uses a gift for
mathematics to create variations in a quilt pattern certainly

reveals her creativity, as Mother did with this design. I call it Mother's Own, because with its combination of lanterns, bars, and overlapping squares, it features some of her favorite pattern elements.

Convincing my mother of her own sense of innovation, however, was not easy. I still remember my shock when she politely announced, "I'm not creative." I remained speechless for a few moments, a rare thing for me. She'd been complimenting my writing, wondering where my

brother and I had gotten our creativity. I was brought to tears by the humility of a woman I admired so much and thought to be the source of my own talent. As most of us are, my mother was her own worst critic. Despite years of quilting, of adapting dress patterns, and of adjusting recipes to her family's needs, she refused to acknowledge that she possessed the same ability to see things in a new way.

Then she began to show her quilt pattern changes to her local guild. The women she held in high esteem praised her skills and her new versions of traditional patterns, especially as she allowed for smaller, odd-shaped pieces, such as the quilts she made for my daughter's wheelchair. "Maybe I am creative," she finally admitted.

It's often been said that our talent is a gift from God, while what we choose to do with it is our gift to Him. Nothing could be truer. When we acknowledge the Source of our creativity, we acknowledge the intimacy we share with the One who created us.

PRAYER STARTER

- - - - - - - - - - - - - -

Lord, thank You for the sense of creativity and wonder You have instilled in all of Your children. Guide us as we seek to use it in ways that honor You and those believers around us. Amen.

The Influence of the Past

TURTLE

Take the things you heard me say in front of
many other witnesses and pass them on to faithful
people who are also capable of teaching others.
2 Timothy 2:2 CEB

With fabric from the 1950s and a pattern from the 1930s, the Turtle quilt spans a lot of years. Granny Bowlin pieced it in the '50s, but the final touches weren't completed until my grandmother Omie took it over in the early '80s. Most of the quilts in my possession took time to complete, but even in my family that definitely sets a record. My mother always pointed out that the Turtle was a true record of how quilting techniques transcend time. What was taught to young quilters in the '30s still works today.

My grandmothers and my mother all wanted me to carry on this tradition of needlecraft, which they felt would continue to be a useful skill no matter how the world changed. They were right, but I couldn't seem to get the hang of it. I took sewing lessons, but caused a lot of sighs of frustration when I managed to put in a zipper backward. Even when I measured my patterns slowly and cautiously (so I thought), the cut pieces wound up too small. I broke needles in sewing machines, and my hand stitching bore more of a resemblance to a snail's trail than a plumb line. Eventually, Mother sent me back to my books.

Yet, despite all the failures, those sewing sessions had a lasting impact on my life, although we didn't recognize it at the time. While I was trying to figure out how to make stitches all the same length, we were talking. Family history. Faith. The normal struggles of life for my mother and my grandmothers when they were children. I heard about the Great Depression, rationing, the boys lost to war. How women held their families together as the men had to go off to look for work, often hitchhiking or riding the rails. My grandmother Omie had lived through four wars and prayed never to see another. Most of all, I heard about the faith and trust in

God that enabled them to get through it all with a sense of hope and wonder for the future.

Times like these, when we share ourselves and our faith with our children, are those that build trust and belief across the years. Conversations about life and faith often happen when we're doing other things, but when our children hear such information from us, they'll understand how vital God and our own families have been throughout our lives.

PRAYER STARTER

- - - - - - - - - - - -

Lord, show us ways to teach our children all they need to know—about us and about You—in order to build a strong foundation for their future. Amen.

Preserving Our Past

CAROLINA LILY

- -

Only take care, and keep your soul diligently,
lest you forget the things that your eyes have seen,
and lest they depart from your heart all the days
of your life. Make them known to your children
and your children's children.

Deuteronomy 4:9 ESV

- -

The news wasn't hopeful. My mother and brother had talked to quilt historians all over the country. They'd been to a museum that specialized in preserving antique quilts. All in hopes of salvaging the Carolina Lily quilt. Constructed in the 1840s in North Carolina and brought to Alabama before the Civil War, the quilt had spent several years buried in a trunk in a barn to keep it safe. But that time underground had started a deterioration that we could not stop.

Bright reds and greens had faded to rust and brown. The white background had turned beige, and water stains circled the blocks. The fabrics were brittle, almost crackling when the quilt was moved, a sign of the threads breaking down. Part of the edges had frayed away, leaving behind shattered strands and tufts of dirty wool. Permanent creases crisscrossed the quilt with dark lines, and the oils of countless hands had left patches of discoloration.

The cost of preserving it? Well above ten thousand dollars, a sum none of us had access to. And that was even if it could be preserved. Some of our friends suggested cutting it up, saving the best sections and encasing them behind glass. But we couldn't. So we made the decision to let it go as a quilt and find a way to pre-

serve it as an artifact of family and local history. We donated it to the local museum, and my mother and I wrote up stories about it for the local paper and a community history book.

It was a bittersweet time, but my mother took it well. As she pointed out, "As long as we keep talking about the quilt, and the history it represents, it'll be preserved in the best way we know how, in the hearts of others."

Scripture reminds us of this often. When believers forget to teach their children what has come before, we drift.

We forget our history and the wonderful things God has done for us. How He has helped us withstand the trials of the ages. And in a time consumed with fleeting news and the casual nature of history online, telling our children stories, loving them, and sharing the past with them may be the only way for our history, our beliefs, and the things we value to make a lasting impact.

PRAYER STARTER

Lord, we praise You for all the good things
You've brought to Your children.
Guide us as we teach our own children,
preserving for them the wonders
You've bestowed on us all. Amen.

A Legacy of Needlework

BUTTERFLY HANDKERCHIEF

- -

She makes tapestry for herself;
Her clothing is fine linen and purple.

Proverbs 31:22 NKJV

- -

When I was twelve years old, my grandmother taught me to embroider. I spent that summer with her, and she tried to find something for me to do that didn't involve romance novels and rock 'n' roll music on the radio. As we were both left-handed (and my mother was not), having Grandmother Ila teach me to sew, embroider, and knit seemed logical.

Only, my fingers weren't as talented or trained as hers. My knitting attempts looked as if a terrified chicken had gotten into the yarn, and after three broken needles, she decided turning me loose with her sewing machine might not be a good option. Any thoughts of teaching me to tat lace were abandoned after being barely whispered.

I did, however, managed to fill a column of cloth with

tiny looped flowers and straight stitches. By the end of my visit, I'd even been able to follow the stencil on two pillowcases, which I kept and treasured until the fabric began to fall apart. I never became adept at embroidery, but it did lay the groundwork for me to take up cross-stitching, which I still do.

That Mother and Grandmother Ila wanted me to take up needlecraft was no surprise. I come from a long line of needleworkers, and they thought I'd be a natural at it. They considered it a prime way for women to provide for their families, which was extremely important to them. In addition to the essentials of clothes and quilts, needlecrafts provided some of the few luxuries these women allowed themselves. My grandmother was born 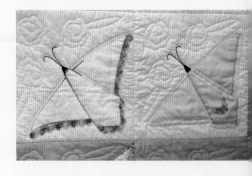 in 1902 and my mother in 1926; both were raised in an era before everything came from the mall. To them, fine handmade lacework or a sweetly embroidered jacket were ways to express the joys and beauty of the crafts as well as the utilitarian nature of them.

It was this joy and beauty that led my mother to want to preserve my grandmother's homemade handkerchiefs, with their gently embroidered flourishes or tatted lace, into a quilt. It was a desire to show where we had been as a family, to display a legacy stitched by numerous women through the years.

The Bible speaks often of the importance of our heritage, of what we leave to our children. Faith and finery are both described as treasures, which demonstrate to our children that looking backward as well as forward is to be held dear. One shows how we value God; the other how we value the legacy of our ancestors. As we honor God and those who have gone before us, we provide a sound foundation for the generations to come.

PRAYER STARTER

Lord, may we honor the "cloud of witnesses" that have come before us and in that they did to provide for our future. Let us never forget their sacrificial work so that today we can thrive. Amen.

Playing Favorites

CHURN DASH

And do not forget to do good and to share with others,
for with such sacrifices God is pleased.

Hebrews 13:16

After my dad died in 1996, my mother lived alone for the next twelve years in the house they had built. Daddy had been the primary contractor on the house, subbing out only the electrical work. So there was a lot of him in it; she was reluctant, to say the least, to give it up. But by 2008, her health had declined to the point where she could no longer care for the house the way she wanted, and remaining alone was becoming risky. She was eighty-two and a forty-year diabetic.

So during one of my trips home, she announced that she'd picked out her assisted living facility and put down a deposit. She'd be moving in May. The scramble started right away, with my brother arriving to help her empty out my dad's workshop and begin the painful process of dividing up the household possessions. Fifteen hundred square feet of house held more than fifty years of memories, which she had to pare down to four hundred and twenty square feet and a walk-in closet.

After she chose her essentials, she turned the decision-making over to us. Mother had never liked to play favorites between my brother and me, but we each had our obvious gifts. He is better with money and business, and he lives in an expansive house. I'm better with instinctual or

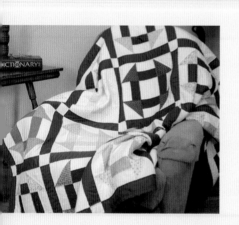

emotion-based decisions, but I lived at that time in a small house. So furniture decisions were easy. He took the pie safe; I took the kitchen chairs.

When it came to the quilts, however, there was more of a debate. These were creations of the heart, many of them by Mother. She selected the ones to move and suggested the rest go to charity. After our furious protests died down, favorites finally emerged. My brother preferred the modern quilts, and picked the ones Mother had made in recent years. I had a fascination with the vintage ones, their stories and the women who made them. I did glom on to the one my father preferred, the Churn Dash.

Neither of us realized exactly how many quilts Mother had stored away, although she'd been determined that I heard the stories about the older ones. When I finally got the last one tucked into the back of my SUV, more than twenty headed home with me. The sadness that followed surprised none of us, since it represented my mother entering the last stages of her life. In the end, the sacrifice was a good thing; my brother and I will preserve the quilts, and the memories will live on to be passed on into our future. In the end, by giving up her quilts, Mother guaranteed that their stories would never end.

PRAYER STARTER

- - - - - - - - - - - -

Lord, sharing sometimes requires sacrifices.
Provide us with the wisdom to make
the right decisions, those that will benefit
our loved ones best. Amen.

Dual Purposes

STORM AT SEA

- - - - - - - - - - - - - - - - - - -

Then they cried to the LORD in their trouble,
and he delivered them from their distress.
He made the storm be still, and the waves of
the sea were hushed. Then they were glad that the waters
were quiet, and he brought them to their desired haven.

Psalm 107:28–30 ESV

- - - - - - - - - - - - - - - - - - -

D o you think, when this is over, I could have something to remember her by? Something she made?"

The request was quiet and filled with pain. One of my mother's best friends, Jo, sat at the funeral home with us during the entire viewing. She and her husband had been the last friends to visit Mother, sitting with her only two days before her death. The loss of her friend, although not at all unexpected, had stunned Jo, and she still reeled from the grief. I nodded, even though the thought of giving up anything of Mother's made me cringe. How could I?

Over the next few days, however, I began to see not

only that I needed to do this, but I realized exactly what I needed to give to Jo. The Storm at Sea quilt was a smaller piece, intended as a throw for a couch or recliner, and it was a lighter weight, so it could be used in combination with other quilts. In fact, I'd been using it on the foot of my bed for the past two winters as a foot warmer on particularly cold nights.

The chaotic pattern appealed to me, especially now, with its dark red stripe to offset different shades of blue.

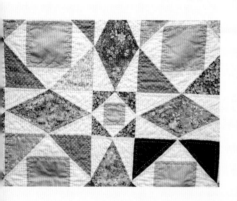

Mother had had a lot of delight putting it together, and it had been one of her favorite pieces. It had stayed on her couch until she moved into the assisted living facility. Now it seemed to reflect the turmoil we all felt with Mother's death. We definitely felt storm-tossed, lost and vulnerable without her. I knew it would be a comfort for Jo, a "desired haven" that might help her find peace. So I packed it up and sent it off. It now has a place of honor in her home, and she's told me that her daughter has instructions to return it to me when Jo dies.

In their own storm-tossed boat, the sailors cried out to the Lord, and He calmed the seas and their fears. When we feel the same, we just need to remember to ask. He will provide whatever we need, just like Mother left a piece of herself to comfort her friend.

PRAYER STARTER

- - - - - - - - - - - - - -

Father God, when we are riding out the storms in our lives, hear our cries for help. Show us how to call on Your strength for peace and wisdom, no matter what we face. Amen.

Separate Hearts

TULIP

When the righteous cry for help, the LORD hears
and delivers them out of all their troubles.
The LORD is near to the brokenhearted
and saves the crushed in spirit.

Psalm 34:17–18 ESV

My beloved Tulip quilt had escorted me into my marriage . . . and it helped escort me out. My marriage dissolved over several months, a time of grief, self-doubt, and depression. I struggled on a daily basis to keep up enough energy to work and take care of Rachel. My husband moved out over Thanksgiving, and we put our house on the market at the end of December. Needless to say, the holidays weren't a lot of fun for me.

I also lost friends during this time, just when I needed them most. But I was a supremely lousy person to be around, whiny and difficult. So I didn't blame the ones who left and was grateful for the ones who stayed. My home was breaking apart around me, and I dragged the Tulip quilt out, often wrapping up in it for comfort as Rachel and I curled on the couch.

Then came the day the moving company representative showed up to do inventory. My husband had taken a job out of state, and his new company was paying for his move. I went around the house with her, pointing out what they would take and what they'd leave. She compli-mented the quilt, amused at how fast I stated that it wasn't going anywhere.

Then, as she prepared to conclude her inventory, she suddenly turned and looked at me. "Are you in a church?"

I stared at her. "What?"

She took a deep breath. "I know you'll think I'm crazy, but God is telling me you need to be in a church. Right away."

I didn't think she was crazy, but it was the first time I'd had someone deliver a message from God. I didn't speak for a moment, and she smiled nervously. "Do you think you need to be in a church?"

As a matter of fact, I did, and I told her so. I started

looking for one that evening, curled up in my Tulip quilt, phone book in hand.

It never occurred to me that God would speak to me through a moving company representative I had met only hours earlier. All I knew and still know is that God hears our cries, and He sends us the people we need when we need them the most. God provides all things, from the amazing to the mundane, to heal our broken hearts.

PRAYER STARTER

Lord, thank You for hearing our cries, for listening to our shattered hearts, for lifting us up when we need it most. May we always hear Your voice and accept Your help. Amen.

From Many into One

POSTAGE STAMP

- -

*There may be no division in the body, but that
the members may have the same care for one another.
If one member suffers, all suffer together;
if one member is honored, all rejoice together.*

1 Corinthians 12:25–26 ESV

- -

It's intricate work that I can't imagine having the patience for. Hundreds of two-inch squares, painstakingly pieced together. Cotton carded by hand. Muslin feed sacks bleached and dyed and sewn together for the backing. Each tiny square is quilted around all sides, an average of seven even stitches to each two-inch side. I get a headache just thinking about it.

The attention to detail has paid off. The Postage Stamp quilt, made for my father in the 1930s by his grandmother, has borne the years well. The cloth, even the muslin backing, is still soft to the touch. While most of the colors have paled, the indigo blues shine as if they were dyed yesterday.

While close examination of the quilt reveals the quality, when I stand back from the quilt, looking at the whole and not just the parts, the real beauty shines through. Patterns emerge, and it's clear that the top is a series of nine-patch constructions. Colors and fabrics move in ebbs and flows from top to bottom. A fabric typically used in work shirts of the period weaves in and out with a deep blue of a dress. Though it might appear to be a random collection of errant scraps upon first examination, it is not. Terah Maude Pope, the quilt maker, put as much attention to the whole as she did the details.

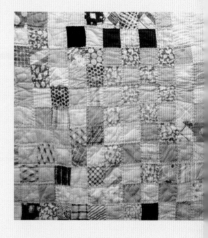

This is sometimes a concept we lose sight of as we go through the busy days of our lives. The calendar for today or tomorrow becomes our primary focus, without thought to how the weeks and months will eventually look in days to come. We get caught up in the "tyranny of the urgent," and we forget to consider the big picture of our future and our faith. While the details, the tiny stitches, make something hold together forever, it is knowing the pattern we want our lives to make that provides real beauty.

PRAYER STARTER

- - - - - - - - - - - - - -

Lord, we are one in Your Spirit and Your love.
Help us remember that believers need to work
together in concert as one body and not separate
from each other in strife. Amen.

Meant to Be Used

BALTIMORE APPLIQUÉ

- -

I know that there's nothing better for them but to enjoy themselves and do what's good while they live. Moreover, this is the gift of God: that all people should eat, drink, and enjoy the results of their hard work.

Ecclesiastes 3:12–13 CEB

- -

There is an ugly pink stain right in the middle of Mother's Baltimore quilt, most likely medicine spilled during an illness. While it unexpectedly matches the other pinks in the quilt, the blotch mars the white cloth, and so far nothing has taken it out. To be honest, at this point, I'm afraid to try anything else.

But that's not the only damage the Baltimore has withstood. Despite curtains and light-blocking blinds, years of the sun's rays from the east have faded its brilliant colors. Many of the appliqués have puckered from being sat on or tugged into place. The precise diagonal stitching started to pull loose a few years before Mother died.

I once asked her why she didn't put it away for safe-keeping, to keep it from being damaged. Her answer surprised me.

"Because I like looking at it. I made it to be used."

Many of Mother's quilts, and certainly all of the vintage quilts, were carefully rolled and stored. She kept white gloves for handling them, and each was aired and rolled in a different way at least twice a year. For those quilts, Mother was a cautious archivist. But for others, like the

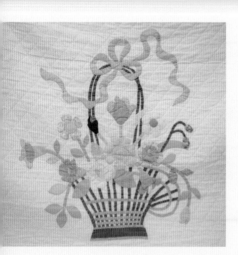

Baltimore, she intended them to be used. The Churn Dash, a favorite of my dad's, graced one of the guest beds until I carried it home with me. Her mother's Cathedral Window covered another. Her Butterfly Handkerchief and the Rosette Basket were displayed in the living room, where she got to tell their stories to any guest who dropped by. "They're beautiful but also useful. They were a lot of hard work. Why shouldn't we enjoy them?"

Why not, indeed? God never intended for us to hide our work under a bushel any more than He wants us to tuck away our faith. He gifted us with creativity, and expressing His gift to us is a way of praising Him. Mother never doubted that her skill with a needle came from God, and she was quick to acknowledge that to anyone who'd listen.

PRAYER STARTER

- - - - - - - - - - - - - -

Father, You give each of us a gift.
Guide us in the use of it, and show us
how to make it useful to You as well
as those believers around us. Amen.

The Value of Family History

TWENTY-FIVE PATCH

- -

When I call to remembrance the unfeigned faith
that is in thee, which dwelt first in thy
grandmother Lois, and thy mother Eunice;
and I am persuaded that in thee also.

2 Timothy 1:5 *KJV*

- -

Tracking down exact birth and death dates for folks in the nineteenth century can be a bit like herding cats. The minute you think you have one pinned down, another pops up across the way. Sarah Jane Rickles, the maker of this remarkable quilt, was born in 1834, 1836, 1838, or 1839, depending on what source is reviewed. The family Bibles say 1834. Her tombstone reads 1838. What is known is that she didn't marry until October 1865, which put her between twenty-seven and thirty-one, quite late to marry during that time period.

There was, however, a war going on. Her husband-to-be, William Franklin Battles, joined the 19th Alabama Infantry on August 19, 1861. The war had only been underway for four months, and they may have decided to wait to marry until he returned. At the time, many thought the war would be short-lived. The 19th Alabama, however, went on to see some of the fiercest fighting of the war, including the battles at Shiloh, Chickamauga, Murfreesboro, Franklin, and Nashville. At Shiloh

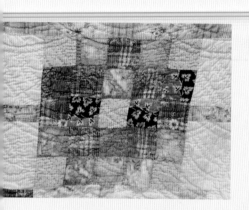

alone, the regiment lost more than two hundred men. That William came home at all is something of a miracle.

But Sarah Jane kept waiting. And believing. The faith demonstrated in this quilt, with its intentional flaws to acknowledge that only God is perfect, illustrates her remarkable reliance on God. She passed this faith not only to her children but to her grandchildren, one of whom was my grandmother Omie. My grandmother was twenty when Sarah Jane died and sixty-one when her own mother—Sarah Jane's daughter Mary—died, and she often spoke about how these two devout women had influenced her beliefs. Their heart for God and their family led her to be one of the most fervent believers I've ever known. Grandmother Omie, in turn, is responsible for some of my own deeply held views. Sarah Jane left behind far more than her quilt.

In our modern and fast-paced world, thinking about the past as removed and remote can underline our ideas of independence and self-reliance. But we never should forget that our ancestors influenced us in many unseen ways, just as we will influence those who come after us. We are all connected, making our faith and trust in God a vital part of our world now, as well as in generations to come.

PRAYER STARTER

Lord, never let us forget that the young people around us are listening, absorbing what we teach them in our words as well as our deeds. Guide us into showing them the wisest paths for their lives. Amen.

For the Future

DUTCH ROSE

- -

Aim to live quietly, mind your own business,
and earn your own living, just as I told you.

1 Thessalonians 4:11 *CEB*

- -

When Grandmother Ila completed the Dutch Rose quilt in 1981, it became the last one she pieced and stitched by herself. After she'd finished the Cathedral Window quilt, she wasn't sure she'd be able to quilt much more, but she went on to complete several, including the quilt she told me was "for the future." When I asked her what that meant, she told me that quilting gave her something to look forward to. A reason to get up and stay up.

She'd been increasingly frail for several years, losing both strength and will. Diverticulitis, which she'd managed to control for most of a decade, also took a serious toll, leaving her in pain many days. She'd been in the hospital for more than one transfusion, and her skin had begun to look papery, bruising easily. Sitting in a chair and doing nothing but watching television became far simpler that trying to keep up her side of the housework, but infinitely more depressing. She hated being a "bother" to my parents, something she worried about more and more as the risk of her falling increased. She just wanted to live quietly, mind her own business, and stay out of the way.

This was the way she'd always lived. Grandmother Ila had not been one to gossip freely, although she did admit to "spreading the news" on occasion. She believed that the best life was one based on Scripture, one dedicated to caring for family and friends and following God's will. She wanted to be useful, to maintain a purpose in how she lived.

Now, after moving in with my parents, she wasn't always able to do so, not as she had done in years past. Quilting made her feel as if she was "paying her way and staying out of the way," as she once put it, and the thought of not being able to continue weighed heavily on her. After the Dutch Rose, she helped quilt a few tops my mother had pieced, but she seldom even dressed. My last photos are of her in a housecoat, unsmiling. By 1983, her health dictated the full-time care of a nursing home. I gave her my little black-and-white television to keep her company, and our limited conversations were primarily about something she'd read in the Bible. We both loved those conversations, with her being the mentor and me the student.

Grandmother Ila's life inspired me in more ways than I can describe, from her taking over her siblings as an eleven-year-old girl to the way she lived her last days. Through all of it, however, she sought to be useful, to have a purpose, and her guide remained the words of the Lord, from whom she'd learned so much and to whom she wanted to give. May we all have such a heartfelt aspiration.

PRAYER STARTER

- - - - - - - - - - - - -

Lord, You are our refuge and our strength.
May we follow Your instructions and Your path
for our lives to the end of our days. Amen.

Relying on Community

FRIENDSHIP

- -

And let the beauty of the LORD *our God be upon us,*
And establish the work of our hands for us;
Yes, establish the work of our hands.

Psalm 90:17 NKJV

- -

This quilt is the work of many hands, and against all odds, it's one of the loveliest in the collection.

I grew up hearing such expressions as "too many cooks spoil the broth," and throughout school, we're urged to "do your own work." Even as crafters and artists, we see praise and recognition given to those who have completed a major project without help. Yet I've also noticed an increase in the number of community art projects springing up, mostly with the goal of bringing people together with a mutual objective. I recently participated in such an endeavor, painting part of a mural that celebrated our community's outstanding features.

Such was the nature of the Hartselle Quilt Lover's

Guild's friendship quilts. When you have more than two dozen quilters contributing to the blocks and the quilting, there's a serious risk—obviously not everyone's skills are the same. A block that's an incorrect size or improperly pieced could throw everything off-kilter. But like an old-fashioned quilting bee, the point wasn't quality; it was community.

The women of the guild loved and supported each other. They prayed together. When they brought the blocks together, ones that had been poorly constructed were taken apart and restitched with gentle instruction or had strips added for sizing. After all, the goal wasn't to demonstrate any one quilter's skill; they wanted to work on a project that would bring them all closer together. And in getting quilters at the local senior center to quilt the final project, the guild brought together even more women in  the community, connecting them over a common purpose. A bonded community stands stronger, with an internal support that can't be shaken.

So it is with all believers. While individual worship and spiritual growth can help grow your relationship with the Lord, it is through community that we receive support and encouragement. Throughout Scripture we are encouraged to gather in His name, not only for worship, but for the strength to be had in uplifting and praying for each other.

PRAYER STARTER

Lord, coming together in Your name provides love, support, and strength we all need. Help us recognize the beauty of each other's work and faith as we lift each other up in prayer. Amen.

The Long Haul

CATHEDRAL WINDOW

- -

Be strong and of a good courage, fear not,
nor be afraid of them: for the LORD thy God,
he it is that doth go with thee;
he will not fail thee, nor forsake thee.

Deuteronomy 31:6 KJV

- -

My grandmother Ila, like most women, disliked grow-ing old. Even when her overall health remained good, she despised her loss of strength, her dependency on someone else to open jars, lift skillets, or move chairs. And she didn't realize that when she took on the challenge of completing a Cathedral Window quilt before her death that it would be the heaviest of all her quilts.

The Cathedral Window, unlike other quilts, has no batting and isn't quilted, per se. Instead, each three-inch square is actually a larger square folded in on itself and tacked down, making a four-layer "frame" for each colorful bit of cloth, the "glass" of the window. When first begun, it's a series of lightweight squares, easily held. When finished, however, each square is five layers thick. It's a heavy coverlet to sleep under, much less to wrestle about during its construction.

As the quilt grew in size and weight, my grandmother prayed about ways to deal with it. Her home had no air-conditioning, and Alabama summers made the quilt unbearable. She set it aside during those months, focusing instead on her garden and canning. With winter's arrival, the idea came to her to put another quilt on her big quilting frame, then drape the Cathedral Window on top, letting only a small portion flow off into her lap. She covered the

rest with a sheet to keep down the dust.

Once when I was asking her about the intensive work that had gone into the quilt, she referred to it as "God's quilt" because "He brought me to it and got me through it. And we talked a lot while I worked on it." Her usual habit was to sing while she quilted. For this one, she'd prayed.

She kept it on her bed for years, then my mother used it

in a guest bedroom. The use can be seen in a slight discoloration along one edge, but the quilt is otherwise spotless. It remains a treasure, a visual reminder of my grandmother's faith, of her trust in God's strength and guidance.

PRAYER STARTER

Lord, You deliver many blessings in our lives, through people as well as treasured heirlooms. Thank You for these, and show us how to build our own faith so that it can be witnessed by those around us. Amen.

All We Need
Is a Bonnet

DRESDEN PLATE

- -

*Let us not become weary in doing good, for at the proper time
we will reap a harvest if we do not give up. Therefore,
as we have opportunity, let us do good to all people,
especially to those who belong to the family of believers.*

Galatians 6:9–10

- -

My grandmother Ila could sew just about anything. In her lifetime she made football uniforms and Barbie doll clothes. She made all of her family's clothes, except the hats, and I'm convinced she could have made those as well. She created bridal gowns to rival anything out of Chicago or New York. Her needlework kept the family fed in more than a few lean times, as she traded work shirts for sugar or flour.

But Grandmother Ila never could have been described as all business. Her tender heart broke whenever she saw someone in need, and she gave away many school clothes, dresses, and quilts to people down on their luck. During the Depression, she fed many a hobo wandering through looking for work. When things got tough for a neighbor, she'd show up with a basket of eggs and milk. She fed my grandfather's farm hands biscuits and ham, and she stretched the resources of their small tenant farm to provide for folks well beyond her family.

Grandmother Ila gave. It's just what she did, and her generosity had an impact on her family and community alike. The Dresden Plate quilt I love so much came to me because I helped her out one summer with the garden and house chores. My grandfather had died two years before, and her farm had been sold. She now rented just the house, tending a small garden out back.

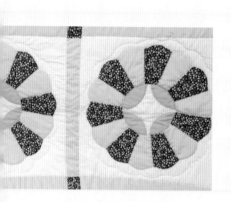

We both worked on the quilt, with a fan under the big frame to keep the air moving during the hot summer days.

Then one day she presented me with a lavender gingham bonnet. The old-fashioned type with a big poof at the back and a large, solid brim. As a young teenager, I was surprised, and a little mortified. It was the most "uncool" thing I'd ever seen. No way was I going to wear that thing.

"You need a bonnet to keep the sun off in the garden. Keep you from getting heatstroke."

A gift, to take care of me. And, yes, I wore it all summer. I just didn't tell any of my friends. But I still have it, that bonnet, a keepsake to remind me how much better it is to give than to receive, to use the work of my hands to help others.

PRAYER STARTER

Lord, our ability to use the blessings You have bestowed on us for the good of others is unparalleled. You give us so much. Help us remember that You provide for us not just for our own sake but for the help of all Your children around us. Amen.

An Artistic Display

OCEAN WAVES

- -

Don't try to make yourselves beautiful on the outside,
with stylish hair or by wearing gold jewelry or fine clothes.
Instead, make yourselves beautiful on the inside, in your
hearts, with the enduring quality of a gentle, peaceful spirit.
This type of beauty is very precious in God's eyes.

1 Peter 3:3–4 CEB

- -

I once tried to dye my hair purple, but the color just washed out, much to the relief of my hair stylist and my mother. I once dressed "goth" for a party, with white pancake makeup on my face, black lipstick, and heavy eyeliner. When Mother asked, "Why?" I told her I wanted to look different. She repeated her question, adding, "Your heart hasn't changed."

My teenage years were a challenge for Mother. Major life changes happened for both of us during those years, and we sometimes turned *on* each other instead of *toward* each other. She had hoped for a somewhat "normal" girl, as she had been. Instead, she wound up with an artistic daughter who hated makeup and dresses, and loved jeans, rock 'n' roll, and beatnik literature. Her friends thought she'd lost her mind when she granted my wish to paint my ceiling blue to match my room's carpet and the walls green. "For sky, earth, and sea," I said. I wanted to run away and join Greenpeace or be an astronaut.

While Mother never quite gave up on making my outside "girly," she began to focus more on my heart. When she discovered me reading the Book of Mormon, she challenged me to explain to her how it differed from the Bible. She asked in-depth questions about my posters that smacked of communism and atheism, and she challenged me to explain why I could value astronomy so much and still believe in astrological charts. Most of all, she reminded me that my ego would be a bigger troublemaker in life than even the most vile of philosophies or wildest of friends.

"Your ego," she announced solemnly, "your pride, is the devil's back door into your soul. Guard your heart. That's where God lives."

Mother made me the Ocean Waves quilt because the undulating pattern of triangles reminded her of my prodigal ways. It was then that I explained that I kept coming back to faith in God mostly because of her. That she continued to walk a devout path had done more to keep my eyes on Him than all the preaching in the world. We both cried, realizing that because she had never given up, we'd finally turned toward each other at last.

PRAYER STARTER

Lord, sometimes we forget how other people view us, how our daily lives influence them. Guide us into being role models more than preachers. Amen.

The Rewards of Perseverance

FLEUR-DE-LIS APPLIQUÉ

- -

Therefore do not throw away your confidence,
which has a great reward.

Hebrews 10:35 ESV

- -

Mother, like a lot of quilters, I suspect, kept more than one project going at a time. When she and my father retired and moved back to Alabama, they built a lovely three-bedroom house that was her basic design—not too big so it would be easy to keep clean, but spacious enough that they wouldn't feel crowded. She kept the two extra bedrooms decorated for guests, specifically my brother and me, but when they weren't occupied, the beds were covered with cutting boards, fabric swatches, stray patterns, and an ever-growing collection of quilting books and magazines.

Storage containers filled with planned quilts took the

place of clothes in to two of her closets. She only quilted one at a time, but if she didn't feel like stitching, she'd pull out another project and pin or sew blocks. Quilting didn't require her to think as much, so she tended to do that during the evening, as her day wound down. Turning a fascinating new pattern to her own design took more mental energy and was more of a challenge.

Mother had always been a morning person, so she tackled that during the morning, when vitality still ruled.

The appliqué quilts, however, broke this routine, especially the fleur-de-lis. Everything about it—from the curves and cutouts of the one-piece appliqué in each block to the intricacy of the quilting stencil she'd chosen— challenged her and occasionally frustrated her. So she would set it aside for weeks, working on something different, which would give her a sense of accomplishment. If I asked how the fleur-de-lis was progressing, she'd usually respond, "Slow but steady, like Aesop's turtle." Despite her struggles with it, she had confidence that she'd finish, because leaving something incomplete was not my mother's way. So she persevered, finally finishing the quilt in fall 1992, just in time for Christmas. When she finally presented it to us after all the presents were opened and the turkey consumed, she was more proud than I'd ever seen her. And she basked in our praise, which she richly deserved.

Scripture is filled with encouragements about persevering in faith, in life, in the tasks set before us. God knows all too well that we get discouraged but that we also are strengthened by that which challenges us. He wants us to have confidence in our own abilities but also in His strength and love for us—He will get us through whatever is set before us.

PRAYER STARTER

Father, thank You for the challenges in our lives that strengthen us and draw us closer to You. May we always have the confidence to persevere. Amen.

Inventive Necessity

TRIP AROUND THE WORLD

- -

Have You not made a hedge around him, around
his household, and around all that he has on every side?
You have blessed the work of his hands,
and his possessions have increased in the land.

Job 1:10 NKJV

- -

Mother and Daddy were only twenty-one when they married, with Daddy being exactly one week older. They'd known each other in school, but he'd dropped out at sixteen to work for the family. Daddy drove a truck, usually taking logs to Florida and returning with produce, and Mother gave up her job behind the drugstore soda fountain to stay home and keep house. They were young and somewhat sheltered, but Mother learned early that she needed to build a hedge around her new marriage.

During that first year, Mother stayed at home while Daddy drove, and she worked with my grandmother Omie to piece and quilt the Trip Around the World. She truly enjoyed getting to know her mother-in-law, learning a new perspective of homemaking and faith. Before long, however, rumors started to reach her about one of her husband's former girlfriends. My dad was handsome and outgoing, and almost completely naïve to the wiles of women. Before he and Mother were married, he once gave two women the same Christmas gift, unaware that women in a small town might compare presents. Even though he extracted himself from that one, he still considered his affable ways harmless.

My dad would talk to a fence post . . . he never met a stranger.

Even after he married, an ex-girlfriend took his ongoing friendliness as continued interest. She'd make an effort to show up wherever he was, implying that his marriage was not really an obstacle to their relationship. As the rumors started to reach my mother, she confronted my father with a choice: "Either you get rid of her or I will." Mother wasn't someone to cross, and my dad made quick work of the former girlfriend.

Mother knew that was only the beginning. After a lot of prayer and long talks with her mother-in-law, Mother made the decision to go on the road with Daddy. The companionship of the long hauls cemented their relationship, bonding them in ways few people understood, and the sacrifice of leaving her home and family was well worth it. She continued riding with him until my brother was born five years later. And the Trip Around the World would be her last quilt until the '70s.

As depicted in Job, God guides and guards those who love Him, but He, in turn, expects us to guard those we love. His Word is filled with instructions, as well as the directions He gives through prayer. After all, anyone we care about is worth holding close, no matter what sacrifice is required.

PRAYER STARTER

Lord, show us Your ways to build a hedge around our families. Help us protect them and prepare them for the world around us. Amen.

A Reminder of Our Faith

OHIO STAR

- -

With all these things in mind, dear brothers and sisters,
stand firm and keep a strong grip on the teaching
we passed on to you both in person and by letter.

2 Thessalonians 2:15 NLT

- -

My grandmother Ila sang while she quilted, unless she had company. She'd been trained, as had my mother, in the Sacred Harp tradition of a capella singing using shaped notes, and she could still hum a complicated alto part without any accompaniment. My mother could do the same, and once I learned the soprano part, we'd often harmonize on one of the church's great hymns. Two of my great treasures from her, in addition to the quilts, are two songbooks. One is her *Sacred Harp* songbook. The other is a frayed and fragile book of hymns and folk songs published in 1915.

Hymn singing is a tradition in my family. Grandmother Ila would tell stories of the extended family gathering on front porches or at church dinners to sing. Everyone sang, whatever the quality of voice. Many of the family played an instrument of some sort, but a cappella singing took precedent, just raising a joyful noise to the Lord. This was especially true during the Depression, when entertainment happened only on the front porch, and hymns reminded everyone of what they had instead of what was scarce.

One afternoon, when I was helping her air and fluff quilts, our conversation turned to hymns, because I'd asked her about her Ohio Star quilt, which she'd made in 1939 from scraps salvaged from feed sacks and work clothes. Grandmother Ila responded to me by reminiscing about life

at the end of the Depression. They saved everything, used everything. Because the quilt is made from whatever scraps she could find, no two blocks are identical in color or fabric.

When I asked about the pattern, she smiled. "Like the Star of Bethlehem. Reminds me that He's always there. Like the hymns we sing. Back then, some of those old boys couldn't read too well. And the King James doesn't exactly make it easy. They got faith from the preacher and the singing. Lots of singing. That's the way we passed things along. One person to another. Lots of front porches in your past. We need to keep reminders in front of us that God is always there. Like the sun. When you believe, girl, when you love God the way we're supposed to, it'll show up in everything you do. Quilting. Singing. Writing. Working. You can't help it. It's in you. It'll come out."

A heritage of faith. A heritage of song. I am reminded of both every time I look at the Ohio Star, a quilt made during hard times with an unshakable faith that God lasts a lot longer than any troubles life can bring.

PRAYER STARTER

- - - - - - - - - - - - -

Lord, we respect the believers who have come before us, who have laid a foundation of faith for us. May we always honor their memory. Amen.

From Crib to Bed to Wall

AMISH DIAMOND

- -

For you created my inmost being; you knit me together
in my mother's womb. I praise you because
I am fearfully and wonderfully made;
your works are wonderful, I know that full well.

Psalm 139:13–14

- -

When my daughter, Rachel, finally had received the diagnosis that would define the rest of her life—cerebral palsy, with a severe seizure disorder—we finally understood why she had been so inconsolable for the past few months. Tactile changes prompted a new round of seizures, and as we tried different meds to regulate the electronic misfires in her brain, we sought other ways to make her comfortable. I lived in T-shirts, the softest material possible for resting her on my shoulder. Blended fabric sheets were replaced with fleece blankets, and the terry cloth pallets she'd used on the couch were exchanged for that pink and blue Amish Diamond quilt my mother had made.

We folded the colors inward to cut down on the stimulation, and the cushiony batting and soft back made a safe place for sleeping. When she grew enough that we worried about her rolling off the couch, we moved the quilt to the floor, where our cats snuggled against her, becoming so protective of her that they would slap anyone who reached for her. My father's German shepherd, Polly, was the same. When we'd visit them, Polly would take her position next to Rachel and never budge. If a stranger got close, the growl from her chest sent them into reverse.

I understood their sentiment. Everyone who meets Rachel, with her blinding smile and irresistible giggle, is instantly charmed. Her helplessness turns us all into guardians. When an interviewer asked me if I thought Rachel, who needs total care and can't do anything for herself, had a purpose in life, I answered, "Sure! She's here to make you think about God. Whether you question why He'd let this happen or praise Him for her beauty, you're thinking about God." I believe this in the very depths of my heart.

Rachel has now lived far beyond any life expectancy offered by the doctors when she was born. The initial suggestion that she would not live past six turned into sixteen, then into twenty-six. The care and love she's received from her family and caregivers has been essential, but we all believe God has wanted her for His purpose as well. After all, He knew what she'd be well before she was born.

When Rachel moved into a hospital bed, the Amish Diamond moved to the wall over her head, standing sentry as surely as the cats or Polly. Mother had made it with prayers, for it to take care of her as long as it could. It's a reminder that with the love and determination of family, anything is possible.

PRAYER STARTER

Lord, You formed us; You know us. Show us our purpose and guide us as we seek to serve and honor You. Amen.

A Simple Nature

SQUARES IN SQUARES

- -

But he's already made it plain how to live, what to do,
what GOD is looking for in men and women.
It's quite simple: Do what is fair and just to your neighbor,
be compassionate and loyal in your love,
And don't take yourself too seriously—take God seriously.

Micah 6:8 MSG

- -

Mother loved this passage of Scripture. She once told me that between this and the Twenty-third Psalm, even more than the Ten Commandments, could keep you on the straight and narrow. She interpreted it as, "Be kind and loving, and always keep God foremost in your mind." She truly believed that if you focused on that, you couldn't wander too far off the path.

Mother liked the simple things. When we'd talk, which was several times a week, she'd nudge me a little about letting my life get too complicated. "You're doing too much. It's not good for the nerves or the soul." And when I'd get too frazzled, which was fairly often, she'd remind me to, "Stop and talk to God about this. He's got big shoulders."

So did she, along with more than the average dose of wisdom and common sense. She followed her own advice, praying frequently when her own life would become more complicated. Once when I asked her why she didn't watch much television, she responded, "I'd rather pray. God's got more to say than the local news."

When I mentioned to her that Rachel needed a lighter quilt for her wheelchair but that I couldn't find one that would keep down drafts but not hold in heat, she surprised me with this lap-sized throw that has a minimal batting and is made from lightweight cotton. She chose this pattern and the bold colors in deference to my daughter's limited eyesight. Rachel loved it and would clutch at it whenever I threw it over her legs. When I asked Mother how she came up with the idea, she just shrugged. "Prayer. About how I could help you."

That was what Mother was about more often than not: walking with God and seeking His guidance in all things, even the small, ordinary things in life. This is what kept her mind focused on helping others, especially her kids. Relying on God helped her be a blessing not only to the two of us but to everyone who knew her.

PRAYER STARTER

- - - - - - - - - - - - -

Lord, may we always turn to You for guidance and help, even in the little things. Especially the little things. It is the simple things in life that sometimes mean the most. Amen.

The Comfort of Warmth

MOTHER'S OWN

- -

I will not leave you as orphans;
I will come to you.

John 14:18

- -

This unusual quilt, which we believe Mother adapted from other patterns, demonstrates her eye for fabric designs and colors, but it also has a bittersweet history. It contains some of my favorite colors—and one of my most excruciating memories.

More than forty years of long-haul trucking had wrecked my father's nervous system. Rigs with worn suspensions and bad springs had worked hard on his back and legs. Cigarettes had played havoc with his heart and lungs. Even though he retired at fifty-seven, most of the damage had been done. He could still do the woodworking that he loved, and he completed most of the carpentry on their retirement home. But vertigo limited his work hours, and as he got older, what's referred to an "essential tremor" or a "familial tremor" made his hands shake.

The result of all this was a need for a calm environment—and control of his surroundings. As his health failed and he became more vulnerable, he would lose his

temper in a snap. His German shepherd, Polly, helped quiet him, and he spent a lot of time in the garage with her, watching the world wander by. His garden also helped, and his plot of land usually produced enough food to keep Mother canning and freezing all summer.

Body and mind are connected, however, and over time, anything unexpected or disturbing could send him into a tailspin of withdrawal and depression. Unfortunately, one of those was my daughter, Rachel. My dad loved her, but as he aged, he became more distressed that he couldn't help her. In a move that broke all our hearts, my parents asked me to stop bringing her to visit.

I felt abandoned, orphaned, and alone. Anger consumed me at first, but I really couldn't blame them. At sixty-eight, my father's physical and emotional health were failing, and he needed to take care of himself as best he could. My mother, likewise. There was nothing I could do to change the situation; Rachel is what Rachel is. There is no "fix" in her life. She is what God needs her to be. Prayer led me to John 14:18, which reminded that I was not alone. We are never alone.

A few weeks later, I received this quilt in the mail. A peace offering from my mother, offering comfort in the one way she knew might work. I did love her quilts, and I knew how much of herself she had put into choosing the colors and adapting the pattern.

But it was that verse in John that helped me make peace with their decision. I continued to visit them alone, but my visits were rare, separating us during a time when my dad was failing the fastest. Nine months after their decision, he was diagnosed with a tumor. He didn't respond well to the treatments. Six weeks later, pneumonia set in, and he died within twenty-four hours.

The quilt, filled with the mix of raw emotions and painful memories, did become my blanket of comfort as grief passed. I mourned, but I was wrapped in the knowledge that I was not alone.

PRAYER STARTER

- - - - - - - - - - - - - -

Lord, may we always remember that You are the source of our comfort in times of mourning as well as our Father when we feel alone. You never leave us. Amen.

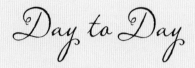

THE LOG CABIN

She looks well to the ways of her household,
And does not eat the bread of idleness.

Proverbs 31:27 NASB

Mother never ate the "bread of idleness." For most of her life, she buzzed with activity, moving from one task to another in a gentle but firm manner. This was certainly true as a young mother, as it is with all women who have lunches to pack and after-school events. But even as a widow in her seventies, Mother began her day with a routine that alerted the neighbors that she was "up and at 'em."

She began her day with coffee and prayer, then she would open the garage door, rain or shine, letting the morning breeze blow the stuffiness from the two-car space. Sometimes she sat in the opening with her coffee, enjoying the morning light. Then it was back to the jobs at hand. She cooked and cleaned, but she also volunteered at the library and the hospital. Even when she rested her body, her mind stayed busy with books and puzzles.

And, of course, quilts. With an empty nest on her hands, she converted one room into a crafter area, with a quilt-sized cutting board giving the bed dual purpose. I never visited her without spotting dozens of triangles, bars, and squares in organized piles, ready for the piecing. Quilts were her great love, and she always had a project in the works. They also may have been her salvation.

Mother had become a widow at sixty-nine, abruptly without her project partner of forty-eight years. She and Daddy had traveled together, worked the yard together. After Daddy had retired, they had spent more than a decade renewing their marriage and enjoying each other. Now, as she struggled to find the "new normal" in her day-to-day activities, quilts became her solace—she once told me she prayed a lot while she stitched, relying on God to get  her through this period. She finished the Log Cabin in 1999, one of the first following my dad's death. It was a familiar pattern, one easier than her previous efforts but a symbol of the rebuilding she'd had to do.

Loss of any sort is a trial, a struggle to get to the next stage in life. Turning to God is not weakness; it's wisdom to rely on the One who can guide us and help us find that new path.

PRAYER STARTER

*Lord, when we've experienced great loss,
hold us close, sharing Your strength
and guidance. Help us find our way again.
Amen.*

One More Time

BOW TIE

- -

Listen with respect to the father who raised you,
and when your mother grows old, don't neglect her.

Proverbs 23:22 MSG

- -

In the ten years following my father's death, my brother and I stayed in touch with Mother as much as we could. All our lives were busy, and distance made it difficult. While I was only 125 miles away from her, my brother lived more than 700 miles away. I tended to make weekend visits, whereas he would come down at least twice a year to help her with house repairs.

Mother was blessed with good friends who filled in the gaps. Charles and Deloice lived across the street and helped with lawn and garden care. They also checked on her daily. Mother's morning routine made it easy for them, especially in the summer. They knew she was up when they saw the garage door open. The house set on a small rise and always got a good breeze, even in the height of summer. Opening the door allowed for a lot of circulation and less heat. It also meant Mother was alive and well and on about her chores.

One morning Deloice looked out and the garage door remained closed. She called and got no answer, so she used the spare key to let herself in. Mother had the flu, and had spent the night alone and in misery. The next few days were a time of introspection and recovery. Mother had always been independent, but she knew the time had come when she needed help. Even at eighty-two, she didn't want to burden friends or family, nor did she want to rely on 911 for help. So she decided to move to an assisted living facility.

Mother loved her new apartment and the staff. But she missed taking care of her house and staying busy. She walked. She still volunteered. But mostly, she quilted. Mother even started piecing a new quilt, a Bow Tie, just before her eighty-sixth birthday. I loved visiting her during those months, watching her meticulous work on each block, usually with a half-dozen pins jutting from the corners of her mouth.

Then came the cataracts, and the surgeries to remove them. She developed a problem in one eye, which she described as "plastic wrap over the lens." She continued to work on the Bow Tie as much as she could, but her eyes gave her more and more difficulty, and her energy waned. She lost weight, dropping to a mere ninety-three pounds before her death. Work on the Bow Tie finally stopped, and I resisted asking about it. That she had stopped quilting was the ultimate sign that she'd made a final turn in her life.

I moved in with her during her final weeks. I wanted to spend as much time as I could with her, to savor this time, to nudge as many memories out of her as I could. I knew what was about to be lost. It wasn't easy to watch her decline, but it was the only way I knew to honor all she'd done for me. As Scripture tells us, taking care of our parents is respect not only them but for God, who has put them in our lives.

PRAYER STARTER

- - - - - - - - - - - - -

Lord, no matter what the quality of our relationship with our parents, honoring them is also a way of respecting You and Your Word. Help us find the best ways to do that in Your sight. Amen.

Whatever Is Old

RIBBON

In old age is wisdom;
understanding in a long life.

Job 12:12 CEB

Sometimes when I mention that my mother left me a collection of heirloom quilts, friends nod and smile. Then I mentioned that some of the quilts are more than one hundred years old, and they frown, surprised that we've been able to keep the quilts safe and looking fresh for so long. Many people I talk to have one or two vintage quilts in their families, and they treasure them, but seldom do more than that. I've often suspected that having the Carolina Lily quilt in our family, with its history and legends, gave my mother and Grandmother Ila a reverence for the art of quilting unparalleled in many of their friends.

After all, quilts were meant to be used, and most were, even the ones in our family. But more care was taken to keep some of them preserved, with a recognition that they were unique—quilts made especially for babies, weddings, housewarmings. Sampler quilts—those first efforts with a needle—deserved recognition. And as our living conditions improved—with regulated heat and air-conditioning—we weren't as dependent on quilts as absolute necessities.

Instead, Mother and my grand-mothers began to see that they were more—they illuminated our family history.

As they got older, family history meant more to them, along with the legacy they were leaving to their children. My mother's wisdom was built on that of her parents and grand-parents, which she freely admitted. My great-grandfather, Oscar Harp, gathered information from every source he could locate. An insatiable learner and continual student of Scripture, he passed much of what he knew to Mother through stories.

My mother adored the ribbon quilt because it always reminded her of those stories, with its patches from dozens of garments. She recognized scraps from work clothes and Sunday dresses as well as remnants left behind from jobs my grandmother had done for others. Sometimes when we'd have the quilt out for airing, she'd point to a square and tell me the background. "Mama made a shirt for Granddaddy out of this before a family reunion. He was so proud." She'd go on to talk about the reunion, naming relatives that she remembered well but whom I barely knew.

The quilts brought out the stories; in the stories there was knowledge and wisdom. Sometimes we get closest to our parents and their faith just by listening—and taking the time to really hear.

PRAYER STARTER

Father, those who have gone before us hold wisdom and faith that we can benefit from, even with our busy lives. May we remember to hear the wisdom and heritage in their words. Amen.

When Women Convene

CAROLINA LILY

- -

Show yourself in all respects to be a model of good works,
and in your teaching show integrity, dignity,
and sound speech that cannot be condemned.

Titus 2:7–8 ESV

- -

In early June 2015, more than a dozen women descended on Ashville, Alabama, to celebrate a quilt. Sisters, cousins, daughters, and nieces, we all had blood in common, even though some of us had not been together in forty years, and some had never met at all. We convened at the St. Clair County Museum and Archives, where the Carolina Lily quilt is stored. As my cousin Mary took photos of the quilt, women who were family but strangers slowly became acquainted. After all, we were there for one purpose. We came together to remember my grandmother Ila and her siblings, primarily her sister Lucille, from whom most of these women had descended.

The family resemblance was present on every face, in

every expression. We could not help but see ourselves, or even better, our mothers and grandmothers, in our new friends' eyes. Some of Lucille's great-great-granddaughters were there, and hearing familiar turns of phrase or seeing hand gestures in these young women presented a clear picture of how family perseveres. And, of course, we told stories, as women will do when they gather. Storytelling is a prized art in my family, and these women were a treasure trove of family lore. We laughed, we joked, we teased, and we cried. We ate a lot of barbecue, and we didn't want to leave. But we had to return to our "real" lives.

Memories, and the pictures, remain, and they remind me of why I began this journey in the first place. While I primarily wanted to preserve the quilts and their stories, even more I wanted a record of the faith and journeys of the women who had made them. So much is lost when a generation of family dies. I wanted to do what I could to keep some of the history alive. The faith of these women is especially vital, because they lived that faith every day, and in doing so, they passed it to the next generation, and the next.

Scripture is clear: When we live as God desires, when we focus on "whatever is noble" (Philippians 4:8), the God of peace will be with you. And the dignity and integrity you establish will guide all those around you.

PRAYER STARTER

Lord, whatever we do and whatever we say is witnessed by those around us, and it impacts them in unexpected ways. May we always live in Your truth and wisdom so that we don't lead anyone astray. Amen.

The Specialness of Everyday Life

ROSETTE BASKET

- -

A wise woman builds her home,
but a foolish woman tears it down with her own hands.

Proverbs 14:1 NLT

- -

My parents were never rich, in terms of money and property. In the first decade of their marriage, money was so tight that they depended on family to help make ends meet. Both of my grandfathers considered credit the work of the devil, and my parents tried to honor that. But when the truck Daddy used to make his living could no longer be repaired, they struck out on their own and got a loan for a new one. A few years after that, Daddy took a permanent job with a trucking company, and their lot got a little better.

Throughout that time, Mother dedicated herself to making their home a warm, welcoming place for not only her husband and son but her friends as well. Used furniture was cleaned and polished until it sparkled. Old quilts became comfortable and attractive cushions. Once, when she was gently washing and starching some of my grandmother's hand-tatted doilies, she explained that clean and comfortable was far more important than expensive and new. "It's about the care and the love, not the money. It's about being there every day, not just when you're needed."

Both my parents lived this concept. Mother saw to the "hearthside" of the home while Daddy handled the physical requirements of the house. They both worked the yard and garden. My father loved my mother's quilts and encouraged her to use them in the décor, although I later realized he wasn't so much a fan of quilts as he was of my mother. In his workshop, Daddy made dozens of hangers and stands for the quilts. He created one specifically for the Rosette Basket wall hanging, and they placed it on the wall opposite the front door. It

was the first thing anyone saw when entering the house, a sign of the welcoming hospitality they offered to all comers.

Throughout Scripture there are instructions on hospitality, which was crucial during biblical times. Then the hospitality of strangers could make the difference between life and death. Even Jesus sent out His disciples without provisions, knowing they would find welcome (Luke 10). Now hospitality can make the difference between a house and a home, between a safe place to rest and gather with family and a building to be avoided. I pray that the lessons my mother taught me always shine through in my home.

PRAYER STARTER

Lord, open our hearts to others, who are also Your children. Show us how to make our homes open and warm, so that we may show Your love to all who come to us. Amen.

A Stitch of Healing

DIAMOND COMPASS

Have mercy on me, O LORD, for I am weak;
O LORD, heal me, for my bones are troubled.

Psalm 6:2 NKJV

In the late '70s, my grandmother discovered that quilting can be more than a passion; it can be healing as well.

After my grandfather died in 1970, Grandmother Ila continued living alone in the house she'd shared with him since 1941. She tended her small garden, cared for the chickens, sewed for the local children, and chatted with two of her sisters, who still lived close. My grandmother had never learned to drive, so most days were spent at the house, although her brother, who ran the local drugstore, would help her run errands and get to church on Sundays.

Grandmother Ila had always been self-sufficient, and she prided herself on her independence. The summer I stayed with her I learned a great deal about how little we really need to thrive and be happy.

All of that changed, however, when her house was burglarized. She came home from church to find all her possessions ransacked. With the house topsy-turvy, it took her a while to figure out that they had stolen money, some personal treasures, and all her weapons. They even took her favorite Bible, which she had left on her nightstand. The burglary shook her to the core, shredding her independence and making her jump at every sound. She couldn't sleep, and she knew she'd never feel

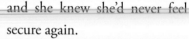

secure again.

After a lot of prayer, she decided to move in with my parents. My father converted our bonus room into a studio apartment, and at seventy-five, my grandmother moved to a new state. She felt safer, but loneliness soon replaced anxiety. She'd left behind her siblings, her church, and her friends. My mother worked a part-time job, and my brother and I had long since moved out.

To pass the time, Grandmother Ila started a quilt, a Diamond Compass pattern, which she found appropriate. "I need something to guide me," she explained. With her old quilt frame taking up much of her room, it felt more like home. And although she'd been reading in our family Bibles, my mother bought her a new one, a large-print that was easier on her eyes. Within a few hours, she started going through her favorite passages and making notes in the margins, transforming the Bible into her own, familiar and consoling. By the end of the summer, Grandmother Ila had found comfort, had settled into her new surroundings. In turning to her quilting and her faith, my grandmother had found her way home.

PRAYER STARTER

Lord, let us remember that You are our true home and that You will always guide us to a path of healing. Amen.

Piecing a New Whole

HEARTS IN BLOOM

- -

Though I walk in the midst of trouble, you preserve my life;
you stretch out your hand against the wrath of my enemies,
and your right hand delivers me. The LORD will fulfill his
purpose for me; your steadfast love, O LORD, endures forever.
Do not forsake the work of your hands.

Psalm 138:7–8 ESV

- -

Although it may not be recognized by the medical profession, quilters have long known that quilting is more than a creative outlet, more than art, more than leaving a legacy. Quilting is also therapy. Piecing a top, layering it, and stitching a pattern through it is a long-term, intimate process. Like a potter on a wheel, a quilter bent over the bright colors knows the smallest details of each square inch, knows where the flaws and perfections are, knows the quality of her work. It requires a focus that shuts out problems and allows a solace to settle over the quilter.

Quilting got my mother through many of the roughest transitions of her life. Her children leaving home, the deaths of her parents, the birth of a premature grandchild with disabilities, and the death of her husband. Mother, as a truck driver's wife, had always been independent. She once described herself as a "single mom with all the responsibilities and none of the benefits," meaning she had to take care of hearth, home, and kids while Daddy was gone, as well as fending off men who saw her absentee husband as an "opportunity." In the last twelve years of their marriage, however, Daddy had been retired, and they'd grown closer than they had ever been. His death left her bereft.

There is no loss equivalent to the death of a spouse. My brother and I tried, but our consolation and company weren't enough. Quilting became her refuge, but it was more than just therapy. It connected her to the very people she needed most— believing women who had experienced the same jarring pain as she had.

We should never underestimate the healing power of a shared faith, a common pain, and a collective hobby. Mother and I both believed that God had nudged her back toward her fellow quilters as a way of giving her the very refuge and strength she needed. He would not forsake her in the midst of her toughest trial.

PRAYER STARTER

Father, You are always by our side,
gently nudging us toward the right path.
Help us recognize Your blessings when they
stand before us. Amen.

That Which Survives

BUTTERFLY HANDKERCHIEF

- -

Give generously to them and do so without a grudging heart;
then because of this the LORD your God will bless you
in all your work and in everything you put your hand to.

Deuteronomy 15:10

- -

Most women of my grandmother's age sewed; they had to. Financial hardships and geographical distance made it almost impossible for folks to traipse off to the stores for ready-made dresses and quilts. But my mother's mom, Ila, also crocheted, embroidered, tatted, and worked as a seamstress in a factory. She made bridal gowns with hand-tatted lace, and truly loved "making it look pretty."

But she seldom used those talents for herself. Ila liked to give, and the hardships of her life had geared her more toward providing for others, beginning with her seven younger siblings following her mother's death. Taking on the household duties and acting as a substitute mother to her brothers and sisters left little time for self-indulgence.

Her one extravagance was her Sunday handkerchief, those bits of cloth tucked away in her purse. Tissues were not yet common, so her handkerchiefs were practical as well as lovely—ready to catch tears, swipe sweat, or clean a child's face of that morning's oatmeal. She made them pretty by choosing florals and adding lace, or a soft linen and embroidering flowers or butterflies in the corners, adding style without interfering with practicality.

When Grandmother Ila died, she left behind a drawer packed with the handkerchiefs. She had so many because she rarely missed church. It's the image almost everyone had of her: Ila in her hat, with her handkerchief tucked in one palm, celebrating her faith every Sunday. No matter how often she moved or downsized, the handkerchiefs remained a treasure. Mother, in turn, found it impossible to get rid of them as Grandmother Ila's possessions were dispersed to relatives and charities. She lovingly tucked them away in her cedar chest.

Then, browsing through one of her many quilting magazines, Mother found a pattern for the

Butterfly Handkerchief quilt. Setting her current project aside, she started work on a quilt that would honor her mother. Her most-prized quilt, it remained on display in Mother's living room until she moved into assisted living, and it was the quilt we used on her casket after she died.

Grandmother Ila inspired without words. Going to church every Sunday. Showing that functional can also be pretty. Working and giving without complaint. Just by being faithful, my grandmother passed on to those who came behind her how to live for the Lord.

PRAYER STARTER

Father, help me remember the witnesses in the faith who have come before me. Allow me to honor them and pass along their true beliefs to others. Amen.

Beyond the Bedroom

PUZZLE

- -

By wisdom a house is built,
And by understanding it is established;
And by knowledge the rooms are filled
With all precious and pleasant riches.

Proverbs 24:3–4 *NASB*

- -

When I was growing up, quilts remained tucked away in bedrooms, usually rolled and stored in a closet or snugly settled between the sheets and bedspreads. The only throws I saw in dens or on couches were knitted or crocheted afghans, and the only fabric decorations were tatted doilies. But as quilting moved from being less about surviving winter and more about being an art, quilts emerged from the bedroom.

Whatever form they took, the quilted pieces in my mother's home were luxurious and comforting. My mother made this Puzzle table runner after a friend gave her a centerpiece clustered with flowers of the same yellow and blue shades. It fit perfectly into her "country style" dining room, adding a visual interest that made the flowers pop even more.

Mother's eye for color and coordination was trained by years of self-study, and she constantly sought to add to that knowledge. Her insatiable desire for learning never waned, even into her eighties. For years, she read more than fifty books a year, and she always asked me to bring her more. When she did watch television, which was seldom, she chose news or documentaries.

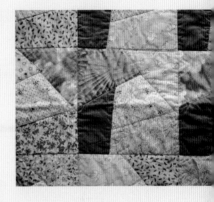

Once she'd gotten past her initial qualms about trying new styles of quilting, she dived in with an eagerness, piling her craft room with new ideas and projects, wanting to discover more. Her experiments often turned into place mats, runners, or small wall hangings, filling the rooms "with all precious and pleasant riches." She also passed her desire for learning to both my brother and me, and she frequently wanted to engage us in conversation about a recently acquired bit of information. When I began to work as a Bible editor in the early 1990s, she quizzed me often about my projects. That she could talk to me about biblical resources thrilled her to no end.

That I can look at one of her quilted works and remember a woman of great faith and inquisitiveness may seem unusual, but that's who she was; her legacy includes those beautiful traits and more. After all, the legacy we leave behind is not just about what we achieve during our own lifetime. It's about the qualities we pass down to those around us, who are affected and changed, and who go on to pass those qualities to others. It's thus that my great-great-grandparents influenced children they would never know in their lifetime. Legacy is made up of who we are, not just what we do.

PRAYER STARTER

- - - - - - - - - - - -

Lord, our ability to influence and impact other people extends further than we sometimes realize. Help us always to reflect You in all our actions and words. Amen.

A Solace in Mourning

STORM AT SEA

- -

No one should seek their own good, but the good of others.

1 Corinthians 10:24

- -

Losing someone you love and have been close to is always a shock, whether or not the death is expected. The grief is immeasurable, and while it may vary depending on your relationship, it can be consuming, with little comfort in sight. Death also brings changes that must be faced, however reluctantly.

Because of Mother's failing health, I was staying with her, sleeping in her room so I could help the assisted living facility staff with her care. On November 11, 2014, I woke about four in the morning. As I lay there, wondering what had disturbed me, I realized I couldn't hear Mother breathing. I got up to check on her. Her body was still warm, but she had gone to be with her Lord. I was numb, but I immediately starting thinking about what she would want me to do next.

Fortunately for me, we'd talked about this. She had been ready, and we had made plans. "Don't be too sentimental. I'll be gone, in a better place. Do what's best for you and Ray and our friends. Make sure everything goes where it'll do the most good."

So that's what Ray and I did. Most of her remaining furniture went to friends who needed it. Her clothes and household items went to a charity that specializes in helping people who've suffered tragedies, such as house fires. Knickknacks, food, and supplies were given to other residents. Most of her quilting supplies went to a fellow quilter

down the hall. I kept her books, recliner, and sewing machine—with a small delusion that I'd someday learn to sew.

Then there were her quilts. My primary solace was in her quilts, which is why I gave the Storm at Sea quilt to her friend Jo. I understood, all too well, the need to have one close to me. The quilts were Mother's heart and a true portion of her legacy. She would want their stories to live on. Already I have more plans for them, to continue that heritage; since my child can't care for and appreciate them, I'm making arrangements to distribute them among my cousins.

I think Mother would be pleased at how closely we followed her instructions to make good use of her possessions; all her life she had looked for the "good of others," whether that was her immediate family, close friends, or desperate strangers. I know, too, that she'd agree with the distribution of the quilts she'd cared for most of her life. She'd cherished them not just because of the needlework skills they revealed but also because they were a connection to family, to her heritage. Her love of family had been embedded in her nature as deeply as any other quality. Making sure that the family history continued to the next generation would have made her happy.

PRAYER STARTER

- - - - - - - - - - - - - -

Lord, turn our hearts to the doing good for others. Let us turn our minds and hearts less to ourselves and more to the benefit of all Your children. Amen.

Bringing It Home

BOW TIE

- -

I have fought the good fight,
I have finished the race, I have kept the faith.

2 Timothy 4:7 ESV

- -

It was over, that long week that included my mother's death, her funeral, and the emptying of her small apartment at the assisted living facility. I had been numb for most of it, dependent on the details and necessary tasks to get me through. Mother's death was not unexpected; she'd been ill for a while. But as a friend of mine once said, "There's a huge difference in knowing it's going to happen and it actually happening. You can only prepare so much."

But preparing did help. Mother and I had talked extensively about what she wanted, about which outfit to dress her in, which quilt to use for the casket. What possessions went to charity; which to friends. Two of her best friends, Jo and Deloice, helped me transport items, and the facility staff was invaluable in getting me through that time.

My brother arrived from Virginia to take over the business aspect of Mother's passing, working with the facility on final bills and government payments. My friends Sunny and Marilee drove from Nashville to help carry items back to my house.

What I wasn't prepared for, however, was the white sack in the top of Mother's closet. Curious, I pulled it down to discover her last quilt. A Bow Tie quilt. I remembered her working on it a couple of years before, but her eyesight and stamina had drained away before she could finish quilting the last few squares and attaching the binding. There

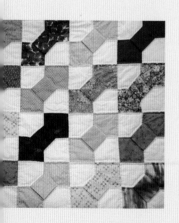

was not much left to do, but she just couldn't do it. I sat for a long time, just holding the quilt, tears on my face. I didn't know what to do with it. I finally packed it up and put it in my car.

I wanted it finished, and at first, I asked Marilee's mother to help. Then I realized I needed to complete it myself. Now, while I helped with my grandmother's quilting when I was a child, I'm not a quilter. But quilting is in my blood, and this was *my* mother. I needed to do this.

Sometimes we really want to let other people do the work we need to take on ourselves, whether that's caring for loved ones, teaching our children about life and faith, or volunteering where we're needed. But Scripture reminds us that we won't be judged on the earthly things we accomplish. Instead, God looks at our heart and how we lived out our beliefs.

My mother passed a lot down to me: her faith, her sense of integrity, her wisdom. I want to honor that in every way I can. And while my stitches may not be as tiny and straight as hers, finishing her final quilt is one way I can say, "You ran a great race. Thank you, Mom. I'll take it from here."

PRAYER STARTER

- - - - - - - - - - - -

Lord, help me remember that one of the best ways I can honor those who came before me is to continue sharing all that they had given to me. Amen.

ACKNOWLEDGMENTS

The community of folks who helped, supported, and encouraged this project along are numerous, and I love them all. My mother's best friends, Jo Owens and Deloice Sanford, made a painful transition much smoother, and continued to check on me and comfort me long after Mother died. My own friends were there for me as well: Marcheta Claus, Sharon Cronk, Marilee Dye, James Minor, Sunny Spain, and Teri Wilhelms.

Most of all, I'm thankful to Pamela Clements, whose eyes lit up when I pitched the idea for this book; Sandra Bishop, who never gives up on me, no matter how many missteps I made and deadlines I miss; and to the lovely folks at Worthy, who made this a landmark in my life.

ABOUT THE AUTHOR

Ramona Richards is an award-winning editor, writer, and speaker and has worked on staff with Abingdon Press, Thomas Nelson, Rutledge Hill Press, and *Ideals* magazine. The author of nine books and a frequent contributor to devotional collections, Ramona has written sales training videos, feature film scripts, novels, Bible studies, gift books, biographies, cookbooks, and magazine articles. Her daughter, Rachel, has severe disablilities and is often featured as the heroine in Ramona's devotions and magazine articles. An avid live music fan, Ramona loves Nashville, which she has called home since she was ten. She can be found online at ramonarichards.com.

IF YOU ENJOYED THIS BOOK, WILL YOU CONSIDER SHARING THE MESSAGE WITH OTHERS?

Mention the book in a blog post or through Facebook, Twitter, Pinterest, or upload a picture through Instagram.

Recommend this book to those in your small group, book club, workplace, and classes.

Head over to facebook.com/ramona.richards, "LIKE" the page, and post a comment as to what you enjoyed the most.

Tweet "I recommend reading #MyMother'sQuilts by @ RamonaRichards // @worthypub"

Pick up a copy for someone you know who would be challenged and encouraged by this message.

Write a book review online.

WORTHY®
PUBLISHING

Visit us at worthypublishing.com

twitter.com/worthypub

worthypub.tumblr.com

facebook.com/worthypublishing

pinterest.com/worthypub

instagram.com/worthypub

youtube.com/worthypublishing